PETER TURNER and PHILIP VOYSEY

Start Your Own Business

BLANDFORD

Thanks . . . .

The authors are extremely grateful for the help received in writing this book, and would particularly mention John Donnellan (Association of Independent Businesses), Graham Lee, (British Insurance & Investment Brokers Association), Norma Roth (Co-operative Development Agency), I.V. Williamson (Co-operative Union Ltd), Paul Derrick (formerly C.P.F. Ltd), Mrs C.A. Trees and Miss B.M. Leighton (Health and Safety Executive), David Ralley (ICOF Ltd), Roger Tidball (Kalamazoo), Mrs Helen Wells (Manpower Services Commission), Irene Jeffrey (Small Business Bureau), Pauline Craig (Small Firms Service), E.F. Richardson (West Yorkshire Fire Service), J. Dryden and Brian Jackson (West Yorkshire Police) and Trevor, of the Co-operative Bank Ltd – twice disturbed in the early hours of the morning by one of the authors who thought he was ringing his son-in-law. Our thanks also to the staffs of the Inland Revenue, HM Customs and Excise, and the Department of Health and Social Security.

First published in the UK 1989 by **Blandford Press**
An imprint of Cassell,
Artillery House, Artillery Row, London SW1P 1RT

Copyright © 1989 Peter H. Turner

All rights reserved. No part of this book may be reproduced or transmitted in any form or by any means, electronic or mechanical, including photocopying, recording or any information storage and retrieval system, without prior permission in writing from the publishers.

This book is sold subject to the conditions that it shall not, by way of trade or otherwise, be lent, re-sold, hired out or otherwise circulated without the publisher's prior consent in any form of binding or cover other than that in which it is published and without a similar condition including this condition being imposed on the subsequent purchaser.

Distributed in the United States by
Sterling Publishing Co., Inc.,
2 Park Avenue, New York, NY 10016

Distributed in Australia by
Capricorn Link (Australia) Pty Ltd,
PO Box 665, Lane Cove, NSW 2066

ISBN 0 7137 2074 3

Typeset by St George Typesetting, Redruth, Cornwall
Printed in Great Britain by Cox & Wyman Ltd., Reading, Berks.

Contents

AN INITIAL WORD
So! You want to start your own business — 1

STARTING YOUR OWN BUSINESS
The preliminary questions — 2

THE FIRST BIG QUESTION
Have you a marketable product to offer? — 7

THE SECOND BIG QUESTION
Can you market the product? — 14

THE THIRD BIG QUESTION
What about premises? — 23

THE FOURTH BIG QUESTION
Stocking up — 33

THE FIFTH BIG QUESTION
Gearing up — 44

THE SIXTH BIG QUESTION
Staffing up — 55

THE SEVENTH BIG QUESTION
What legal format? — 64

| THE EIGHTH BIG QUESTION | |
| *Going for the big time?* | 74 |

| THE NINTH BIG QUESTION | |
| *Finding the cash* | 81 |

| THE TENTH BIG QUESTION | |
| *Accounting for the cash* | 90 |

| THE TENTH BIG QUESTION CONTINUED | |
| *Some particular accounting problems* | 102 |

| THE BUSINESS PLAN | 114 |

Dedicated, with love, to Joy

AN INITIAL WORD:

So! You want to start your own business

Well, why not? Maybe you feel you have a good idea which will net you a fortune if you market it properly – or maybe you are just fed up with the limitations, and frustrations, and 'aggro' of working for someone else.

Most men and women of any spirit feel, from time to time, the urge to 'have a go' at becoming a captain of industry – or just to run their own firm quietly in their own way without having to say *Yes Sir* and *No Sir* and *Three Bags Full Sir* to some benign idiot who really doesn't know whether he is coming or going, and whose job you could do much better anyway.

Many have, in fact, 'had a go'. Some have been only modestly successful, even if successful at all. But others have hit the jackpot.

A great number more would have been successful if only they had set about things in the right way – and asked themselves the right questions before they started.

Others – again if they had only faced up to the right questions early enough – would probably have never started. If nothing else, they would have saved themselves from an immense amount of anguish, trouble, and bitter disappointment — and would probably have avoided losing a lot of their own (and possibly other people's) money.

This little book sets out the important questions which you should ask yourself if you are thinking of starting your own business. It helps you to assess whether your ideas are feasible, and guides you in the preparation of a Business Plan – an essential first step in setting yourself on the route to making your first million (well, perhaps, your first few thousand).

STARTING YOUR OWN BUSINESS:
The Preliminary Questions

Before we get down to detail, let's take a preview of the general situation.

Initially, take an honest look at yourself and ask:

Exactly why do you want to run your own business?

This question is more important than you might think, for it raises the important question whether running a business will give you what you want.

Many people, unfortunately, have quite unrealistic ideas about the pleasures of being their own boss – ideas which are more suitable for Cloud-cuckoo-land than for the real world.

The question is also likely to be a difficult one. This is because the real reason may lie deep down in your subconscious. It may require some real soul-searching to find it. The true answer may well be quite different from the one you imagine as you walk down the road on your way to spend yet another day working for someone else.

If 'doing your own thing' is likely to provide you with what you want from life, and *if* you are prepared to face up to the challenges involved, and *if* you can avoid all the pitfalls along the route, then – and only then – will you be likely to succeed.

And if you do succeed, the rewards can be very considerable indeed. Not only cash-wise, but also as regards self-satisfaction and personal achievement. So, we come back to the question: *Why do you want to run your own business?* Let's consider some of the possible answers.

No future in present job

Fine, but are you sure that you are simply not going

through a temporary – though possibly prolonged – bout of depression? Are you equally certain that there will be a more exciting future for you in 'doing your own thing'? The path to riches is paved with failures.

The rewards (pay, job-satisfaction, chances of promotion) insufficient in present job

But will you be willing to work for very long hours for dismally small returns – at least for the first few years? Most people who have not tried running their own business do not realise just how demanding it really is.

Worry about insecurity of the present job

Nobody likes insecurity, particularly if one has a wife, children, dog and a heavy mortgage to support. If this is your concern, would you not do better to seek a safe job in the civil service or something? Running your own business must be one of the most insecure jobs in the world – just think of the number of times you see small businesses in the High Street change hands.

Just fed up with working for someone else and with its associated constraints and restrictions

Running your own business will certainly give you the chance of doing what you want – but remember that if you have to borrow some of the capital, you may well find other people wanting to have a say in what you do with it – and wanting a cut of the profits to boot.

Unemployed anyway – creating one's own employment is a way of providing for oneself what present society is unable to provide

OK – but remember that all the worry, the insecurity, the commitment of money and time, the need to have an 'idea' which will 'go', and all the stress and strain of doing your own thing, means that being your own boss is *not* a panacea to end all ills.

4 START YOUR OWN BUSINESS

Have a good idea for making money – own business is the best way of exploiting it

Again, excellent – provided you have done your homework and are satisfied (a) that it *is* a good idea, (b) that it *will* make the money you think it will, and (c) that it is within your ability and resources to do anyway.

If none of these reasons fit your case, then what is it that makes you want to be your own boss? See if you can write it down as a clear and precise statement. Do you honestly consider that running your own firm will be the answer?

Running your own business can be immensely worthwhile and rewarding. But, as with everything else in this life, you cannot have the goods unless you are prepared to pay the price. So ...

What is the 'price' you must be prepared to pay?

First, there is *the amount of work involved*. Anyone – and there are some – who thinks that being the boss-man of a successful firm means that you can go into the office at ten, and leave by three, having had a sumptuous business lunch in the meanwhile, has a sadly misconceived idea of what it is all about. All who have started their own firm will tell you that it means working – and working very hard – for all the hours that God gives. And this particularly for the first few years, with not so much difference in later years.

Are you really prepared to give up what leisure time you have enjoyed in the past?

Second, it will mean *on-going stress and worry*. The stress factor in small businesses – where the one-man proprietor has to shoulder the responsibility for everything – is far higher than in any other type of firm. As an employee in someone else's firm, most of the worries are not yours; if you were a director in a large multinational, many of the stressful responsibilities would be borne by other colleagues with specialist skills in the fields concerned. But the small man has to be jack of all trades when it comes to management, and shoulder the responsibility for the lot.

Can you take that sort of stress and worry?

THE PRELIMINARY QUESTIONS 5

Third, have you got – or will you be able to raise – *the necessary capital*? Not only the money with which to start the business, but enough to keep it going afterwards? Many, many businesses fail simply and solely because they are underfunded – or, to use a technical term, because they have insufficient working capital. Although there are various sources of capital available if you do not have sufficient of your own (and we shall be looking at them in some detail later), they tend to be both difficult and expensive to obtain if you do not have a successful 'track record' of having run a successful business for a number of years.

To what extent is money likely to be a problem?

Fourth, can you *handle and get along with people*? And here we are talking about some people who can be very difficult to handle indeed. Running a business inevitably means relating to people, whether they be employees, suppliers or customers, and working through them, with them, and (in a sense) for them. If you are one of those who just cannot work along with other people, then there's no way you will succeed in management.

It may involve a bit more than simply being nice to them. It may mean making some very hard decisions.

> *Could you, for example, bring yourself to tell a family man who has served you well for years, that you no longer have a job for him? Particularly if you know full well that there is no other job for him to go to?*

If you can't, you may well find that it is your business, as well as his job, that goes to the wall.

Fifth, will you be prepared and able – physically and otherwise – to work all those *long hours for miserably small returns* – bearing in mind all the deprivation that it will mean for your family?

One thing you will need beyond all others is the sympathy, the support (one could say the devotion) and the active co-operation of every member of your family. It is one thing for you to be prepared to work long hours for a pathetically small income, but will the wife and the kids be able to cope with it?

Many businesses fail because of lack of support from the family. Will you have the support of yours?

The above points must all be given very serious consideration. There is no sense in committing yourself to a venture when it should have been obvious from the start that it could only end in failure – and at the cost to you of a considerable amount of pride, time and money. Rather than to start and fail, it is no doubt better never to start at all.

But if, after having looked at the situation fairly and squarely, you decide that you've got what it takes, that you are prepared to face all the challenges which it involves, then why not have a go? The rewards – personal as well as financial — can be immense. And do not worry if what you have in mind seems to be small, unsophisticated and amateur.

Remember, even the tallest oaks from small acorns grow.

THE FIRST BIG QUESTION:

Have You a Marketable Product to Offer?

There is little point in setting up your own business unless you have decided what business you intend to do. In other words, *what – precisely – do you intend to offer your customers or clients?*

And, secondly, *do they want it?*

These questions are vitally important because unless you have a pretty clear idea of the sort of goods or services you intend to offer, then you cannot even begin to consider the other important questions which have to be faced before you start – such as how much capital will you need, what type of premises, or where would be the best location. Also, unless there is an effective and positive demand for whatever it is you intend to offer, then your net profit at the end of the day is going to look a bit thin.

You may have already decided on what product, or service, your firm is to be based. The identification of this area is, indeed, the first step – and a vital one it is – but it is not sufficient in itself. The next question which must be asked is: *Is it a marketable product?* That is, do people *really* want it (not, do you think they should want it, which is a different question). Will they not only be prepared to buy it, but to buy it *from you?* Will you, in fact, be able to produce it and distribute it – possibly in the face of very stiff competition?

So, the first thing to do is to decide on a product which WILL sell.

In order to succeed in your own business, you do not have to have some new, revolutionary product or idea which is going to set the world on fire. Indeed, such a product could have its disadvantages – the expense and difficulties involved in making people aware of the product, of building up a demand for it, of creating a new distribution network from scratch, may well require far more resources than you can muster. It could also involve an unacceptably high level of risk. You may well stand a better chance by concentrating on a product or a service of which the public are already well aware and for which there is a known and proven demand.

Nevertheless, to stand much chance of success, you will have to have something 'going for you', or to have spotted a 'vacant niche' in the market which you can exploit. This may, for example, be your choice of location – perhaps a new housing development has opened up a possibility for a street corner stationer, or an off-licence, or a video hire agency (but remember you may not be the first to think of it and someone may already be ahead of you in the planning stage). Or you may think you can undercut competition price-wise (but, be careful, low prices usually mean low profits unless you have a very large turnover and you may find yourself working every hour of the day for a pittance). Or you may think you have special expertise which will mark you out from your competitors (but will the public recognise and want that experience?). Perhaps you feel that in an area dominated by massively large and impersonal combines, being small will be beautiful – maybe it will, but the large combines can be very impersonal when it comes to gobbling you up as soon as you pose a threat to them.

Ideally, you want to be offering something at least a little different from your competitors. And you need to be in a growth market – certainly not a declining one.

In addition, you must understand – or at least be both able and prepared to find out – everything about the service or products you intend to offer. You *must* be reasonably certain of a sufficient 'cash-flow' (flow of actual cash coming into your firm) over your first few months, possibly your first few years, of trading. It is nice to be selling vast quantities of goods on credit, but that doesn't pay the rent and the wages at the end of the week. The pressures will be on you all the time to grant credit: you won't find it so easy to obtain it. You will probably be wise to avoid areas where there is already a strong 'brand loyalty' to existing suppliers, for this will be very difficult to break into and to establish an image for your own product or service. Another cautionary note: it will also be as well to avoid areas which are dominated by just one or two very large and powerful suppliers – particularly if they have some control over supplies as well as over outlets. Above all, avoid getting yourself into a situation which will involve a price war with established suppliers – you just won't have the resources to succeed.

WHICH PRODUCT OR SERVICE TO OFFER!

If you haven't already got something lined up, of what sort of business can you be thinking?

In a small book of this sort, it is impossible to offer a comprehensive list setting out all the possible opportunities you might consider. But let us have a quick look at just a few of possibilities.

The first group of possibilities cover the provision of professional or semi-professional services. If you have a particular qualification – such as in accountancy, engineering, architecture, surveying, management and finance consultancy, physiotherapy or the other paramedical fields, to name but a few – you may find that it could form the basis for a business or a practice of your own.

But you must be careful and make extensive enquiries beforehand.

Have you, for example, the *right* qualification for the service you propose to offer? Not all accountants, for instance, can audit company accounts. Do you need a practising certificate from your professional body? Are there legal restrictions – such as the approval and registration requirements necessary under the Financial Services Act – before you can offer the service you have in mind? Will you need special insurance – such as professional indemnity against claims for negligence?

Above all, you must be very careful not to suggest that you are qualified in a way in which you are not: apart from the possible actions for misrepresentation – even fraud – you may find yourself caught under the Theft Act (for 'obtaining pecuniary advantage by deception', to use the quaint language of the law).

A second major group of activities which could form the basis of a business of your own arise from any special skills which you may have – such as in joinery, plumbing, building, TV servicing and repair, secretarial services, translating services, horticultural work, dressmaking, hairdressing, pottery and so on. Again it may be necessary to pay regard to the law – it is now an offence, for example, to offer driving tuition unless you are approved by, and registered with, the Ministry of Transport. Also, you must check very carefully that you do, in fact, have the level of skill which is required: if you are going to work as a professional, you must be up to professional standard. Being 'good' at DIY does not make you a joiner.

A third large group of possibilities, which might be easier to enter if you have no existing qualification or previous experience, is selling – either as a freelance 'rep', a mail-order agent, or a shop-based retailer or wholesaler. There are even opportunities (if you know what you are doing) in the import/export area. But again you may find that you need a special qualification — such as in pharmacy or opthalmic work. In any case, you may well end up with burnt fingers unless you are prepared to get some experience beforehand of the particular area you intend to enter.

One of the problems in entering conventional retailing is the amount of capital you may need 'up-front' – enough, for example, to purchase or lease premises, possibly in a high-rent area, and for an extensive range of stock and fittings. Against this, retail trading usually has the advantage of an immediate cash in-flow as soon as you start trading.

A fourth area which might be worth considering – it overlaps with general retailing in many ways – is hotel and catering work. This involves everything from the modest 'bed and breakfast' service up to the fullblown hotel, and everything from the corner café to the sophisticated restaurant. You may, or you may not, need special training depending upon the type and professional level of the service you intend to offer, but such training can usually be obtained if you are prepared to look around for it.

In retailing as in all other types of operation, extensive enquiries and investigations are necessary to find out just what the job will involve, and what facilities are available to help you meet the requirements of the particular trade-area you are considering.

A fifth area concerns manufacturing and engineering. Here, very different considerations arise. Almost certainly, specialist knowledge and a high degree of technical skill will be needed. Then there is the expense of the equipment – this may well be considerable. Another problem could be the finding of premises suitable for the type of operation in mind. As with all businesses, planning permission will be necessary – but it may well prove more difficult to obtain it for a noisy, dirty industrial establishment than for the simple neat, clean offices of, say, an accountancy firm. Care will have to be taken to research the legal side: the provisions of the Health and Safety at Work Act will have to be strictly complied with; there may be demanding safety standards which both the product and the workplace will have to satisfy; care will have to be taken not to breach any existing copyright or patent rights.

FROM SCRATCH, OR NOT FROM SCRATCH?

So far, we have been assuming that you will be starting your business from scratch. Two ways exist if you want to get a headstart over those who will be doing 'their own thing' right from the beginning.

The first of these is to buy an existing business. This at least solves the question of choice of product for you: the only problems are finding the capital (you will almost certainly have to pay something for the 'goodwill'), and whether you'll be able to cope with running the business once you have bought it.

The major advantage of buying a 'going concern' is that it will have – or should have – an established list of customers and there will therefore not be the same problem or risk in establishing and building up – probably slowly and painfully – a viable demand for one's goods. But, of course, existing businesses are not given away: the vendor of the business will expect to be recompensed for the 'goodwill' which he is handing over – that is, for the established reputation of the business and its value as, in fact, a profitable and going concern. This, of course, will be in addition to the sum he will want for the premises, equipment and stock. The estimate of a fair price for goodwill is a difficult and complex calculation, and it is one on which an intending purchaser *must*, if he has any sense at all, take independent, professional advice.

The second possibility which might be considered is the taking of a franchise. This means the right to sell or produce a well-established product or service under a nationally – sometimes internationally – known name. Examples include Kentucky Fried Chicken, Dyno-rod, Prontoprint, British School of Motoring, Silver Shield Windscreens and Wimpy Bars. The major advantage of the franchise system is that, immediately, the intending business man has a tried and tested product to offer. The franchisers usually provide both initial and refresher training, give help with premises and fittings, allow the use of their (well-known) logo, supply (at a price) stock, and give exclusive rights to the person taking on the franchise to trade in their name over a certain territory. There will be help with obtaining and equipping suitable premises, and advice on advertising and promotion. But again a price has to be paid for the privileges; there is usually a hefty initial franchise fee payable together with a quite substantial ongoing commission based on turnover. Also, the firm granting the franchise usually retains certain rights of control and supervision, with the result that there may not be quite that element of 'being your own boss' which many people look for when starting their own firm. Also, care should be taken to check out the commission or royalty which the firm granting the franchise may want on any 'subsidiary' services or facilities which might be offered – such, for example, as on the proceeds from juke boxes and 'slot' or other machines for drinks, cigarettes and similar items.

This section has contained but a few suggestions for identifying what might, for you, be a marketable product or service. You might pick up a few more ideas by thumbing through the *Yellow Pages* or a local business directory (your local reference library should have copies available). Also, keep your eyes and ears open as you go about town – you will be surprised what ideas occur through chance, as it were, falling on a prepared mind.

But, at the end of the day, the onus must ultimately be on you to come up with something worth doing. If, after considering all the possible lines of enquiry, you are still unable to dream up a few positive proposals which will be worth further enquiry, then – with all due respect – perhaps you should not be thinking of going into business on your own account in any case.

THE SECOND BIG QUESTION:

Can YOU Market the Product?

Although your first requirement in starting a successful business is to identify a product or service which you are *able* to offer, an equally important consideration is to determine whether or not you will actually be able to sell it.

There is, after all, no point in having the most useful product on earth unless

(a) there are potential purchasers for it, and

(b) those potential purchasers can be persuaded to buy it.

This means that, having identified a product or a service which you consider yourself capable of producing or offering, you must ask yourself:

What actual evidence is there that it will sell?

Finding the answer to that question is the first step in what is known as *market research* — that is, looking at the market and deciding what the demand is likely to be and in what way the product can best be sold.

Estimating potential demand for a product or a service is never an easy task, and it is one which is particularly difficult for a potential 'small business' man with the limited research facilities open to him. But, if you want your proposed venture to be a success, it is essential that you carry out the exercise, and dig up just as much evidence as you possibly can.

This could save you from making some very costly and painful mistakes. It could mean the difference between mounting a highly successful business on the one hand, or a miserable failure on the other.

Also, if you decide to seek financial help from one of

the various agencies or banks which help people to establish small businesses, then some sort of firm evidence that there is likely to be a demand for your product is the first thing they will expect you to produce. So, where to start?

The first step is to decide what sort of information you need – then, of course, to look around and see if it can be found. Having ferreted out as much as you can, you should write it up as notes for your initial business plan.

The questions – and the answers – will vary to some extent depending upon the type of business you intend to start, and the particular situation you are in. In general, the sort of information you should look for is the following.

• *The level of competition*

It is essential that you check on the number of firms which will be competing with you. It is important to find out the number, size and style of existing firms and – if possible – ones likely to start in the near future. If there is likely to be serious competition, the question immediately arises: will there be room for you, too?

If there are no competing firms, then the question as to why there are not must be faced. Does it mean that there is, in fact, no demand in the area for what you propose to offer? Have others tried and failed? If you are satisfied that there is a need for your product, how difficult is it likely to be to make consumers aware of it, and to build up the demand for it?

The *Yellow Pages*, local business directories and town guides are good sources of information. The local chambers of trade and commerce, also, may be able to help. Most local authorities these days maintain an industrial or small businesses advisory unit which will be only too pleased to give a sound and unbiased view of the prospects.

If you are thinking of operating on a national rather than a local level, the problem becomes more difficult. Trade journals will probably give some insight, and there may well be a trade association which can give you information and advice.

You may also be able to obtain very sound and helpful advice from the Small Firms Service and from the Rural

Development Commission Business Service (formerly CoSIRA, Council for Small Industries in Rural Areas). The phone numbers and addresses of their local offices can be found in your telephone director.

The level of demand

Obviously, you must make some sort of realistic estimate of what the demand for your product is likely to be. Without going to all the bother and expense of a detailed consumer survey (which would almost certainly be beyond your resources), this is likely to end up as a bit of a guestimate rather than an accurate calculation; therefore, you should err on the side of conservative caution. However, it would certainly be worth while to look at your competitors to try and get some idea of how well (or otherwise) they are doing.

It may also be worth your time to look at similar firms in other areas. But be careful, the customers in other parts may well be different from those in the territory in which you intend to operate – they may be of a different social class, with different outlooks, income levels, attitudes and philosophies. What sells in the north of England, may well not sell in the south. What will be popular in an area with a predominantly young population is unlikely to sell well in an area where the majority are (to put it gently) 'ageing'.

Is the market situation likely to change in the near future?

What is in demand today may well not be in demand tomorrow. We live in a changing world, and the successful business man is the one who can come to terms with those changes.

If you intend to operate locally, you should check whether there are likely to be any major changes in that locality. Is there likely to be a shift of population – are people moving into, or out of, the area? Are any new, vast housing estates planned? Is the age structure changing? Are any new industries expected which will radically transform the nature of the area? Is a new motorway planned which will carve its way right across your proposed territory, or perhaps a major by-pass which will change its whole character?

More particularly, are any firms which are likely to be your competitors likely to move in? You would look rather silly setting up as a small street-corner grocer if a large supermarket is about to open right next door.

Go and look around your market area. Get into conversation with people who might know – the local landlords, for instance and existing traders. Also, people living in the area – both new arrivals and the 'old 'uns'. In particular, check out with the planning department of the local authority what is on the books for the future. They will know and will be pleased to advise you. Again, the local council's industrial development unit should be able to give you invaluable advice.

On the 'product development' front, check on the likely technical developments and changes which are likely to take place. Trade journals are probably one of the best sources of information here, together with anyone you can find connected with the product.

Remember, the world we live in is a changing place.

The firm's 'image'

It is vital that potential customers should be 'attracted' to your firm or product even before they know what it is; certainly before they have got round to examining it and possibly testing it – for unless that attraction is there, they are not going to get round to looking at it closely anyway.

One of the most important aspects to consider is the name – both of the firm itself, and (if applicable) of the particular product or products being produced. There is no need for an immediate decision on this, but it is something which will have to be sorted out before you start business and the sooner you get thinking about it the better. Also, it is likely that it will, again, be a case of chance falling on a prepared mind, and a brilliant inspiration can occur in the early planning stages as easily as in the later.

The name of the firm may be that of the proprietor or partners which, whilst not particularly imaginative, possibly suggests an element of integrity on the part of the owner concerned. Alternatively, it may be a trade or brand name which will clearly distinguish the firm or product from others, and which may suggest something of what it is all about.

Closely associated with the name is that of some sort of industrial design or 'logo' which can quickly catch the consumer's eye and which will come to be associated with the product or firm concerned. This may take the form of the firm's name written in a particular style, or a monogram of its initials, or an abstract design which often seems to bear no relationship to anything. To have a logo has become quite fashionable in recent years; whilst one can question the value of many of them, others certainly fulfil a useful and valuable function and become an important factor in the firm's advertising and promotion.

Names and logos bring up the question of the firm's stationery – letterheads, billheads and the like. Obviously, names and logos will be repeated on these. It is important to consider the general design of the stationery and its quality. The more impressive the design, and the better the quality of the paper, the more expensive it will be – and it can work out as very expensive. The small firm may do well to consider a modest outlay on this item in the first place. Nevertheless, having said that, many small business owners have commented to the authors on how significantly 'quality' stationery affects the attitude of the recipients. A poorly typed letter on cheap paper with badly printed heads can immediately brand the firm as 'rubbish' and not worth bothering with.

In addition to the name and logo of the firm itself, the choice of the 'packaging' of the product is important. In addition to an attractive name, the shape, design, colour and general appearance of the product all have an immense psychological effect on customers: colour of packaging alone has been known to determine whether the product itself is thought to be 'excellent' or 'useless'. Quite irrational, of course, but that's the way our frail minds work.

Distribution

Having produced a product which you feel certain will sell, and having planned out an exciting 'image' for the firm and

CAN YOU MARKET THE PRODUCT? 19

the product, the next thing you will have to think about is how you are going to get the goods (or whatever it is you are offering) from you, to the customer. There are various options open to you; these are known in marketing as the *channels of distribtion*.

Which channel you choose will be determined, to a large extent, by the nature of the product or service you are offering. If you are offering a 'direct service' – such as insurance services or management consultancy, or if you are taking over a retail shop, there will be no 'distribution' as such to worry about in any case: your only problem will be that of letting people know, one way or the other, that you are around. More difficult problems arise where you are producing in fairly large quantities one particular product which you hope to market over a wide area, possibly nationwide.

One possibility will, of course, be to open your own shop at the same time as establishing your manufacturing unit. This has obvious advantages – and disadvantages. Another will be to sell through the existing retail trade, using the shops of others. This will save you a lot of capital investment, staffing and organisational problems, and will give you a much wider spread of market. Nevertheless it will cost you much shoe-leather and letter writing to get your outlets organised, and you will have to allow for the retailers' own profit margins in the price of the goods.

Another possibility would be to work on a mail-order basis – in a sense set up your own retail outlet through the good services of the post office. This can be a very attractive option, but the cost of the necessary and on-going advertising should be borne in mind, together with the ever-present difficulty of ensuring that your promotional material actually reaches a reasonable number of your potential customers.

Advertising

Associated with the problem of distribution is the question of what advertising will be necessary. This will have to be considered under two heads:

(a) What initial advertising will be necessary to establish the firm or the product in the public's mind?

(b) What 'on-going' advertising will be necessary to keep the pot boiling?

Again the nature and style of advertising will, in part at least, be determined by the type of product. It may range from bills and posters, leaflets direct to houses, through local or national press adverts, to full scale TV advertising – which, of course, can be very expensive indeed.

The actual style of your advertising campaign can be worked out in detail as the launch date of your firm gets nearer. What is important at this stage is to appreciate its importance, to begin thinking how you are going to set about it, and to allow sufficient for the cost of it when you come to plan out your requirements for capital.

Volume of production

Finally, it is important to give early thought to the question of your ability to cope with the volume of production or turnover which might be necessary, and the demands this will make upon your capital, storage space, and indeed your ability simply 'to do the job'.

Nothing is as damaging to the long-term interests of a firm than the inability to fulfil orders – and nothing is as galling to the proprietor as the profits he loses on those orders. On the other hand, to be geared-up for a level of production or service way beyond what actually results is obviously immensely wasteful of materials, storage space, capital and of all sorts of other things.

Apart from the importance of 'getting it right', many other items on which decisions will have to be made depend on the level of production which you anticipate undertaking. Therefore, a very careful and detailed estimate must be made, very early, of:

(a) the level of production or service you are going to aim for initially;

(b) what flexibility there will be within your firm for expansion or contraction of the production level;

(c) what storage and other problems might arise if, initially, you overestimate demand.

CAN YOU MARKET THE PRODUCT? 21

TOWARDS YOUR BUSINESS PLAN

At this stage, you should begin collecting information and setting your ideas out for your Business Plan.

Obtain a sectionalised file, and give each section a title relevant to each of the main sections of this book.

Keep your answers and comments to the points itemised below and in other Business Plan sections in the appropriate section, together with any other relevant information – articles from newspapers and magazines, trade handouts, notes on relevant television programmes, pamphlets etc. from government agencies, references to books and other relevant reference material, ideas of your own – that you can muster. You will be surprised at how quickly an extremely useful collection of background and resource information will build up. If you cannot answer the point at this moment, note it as one to come back to later.

Keep the earlier information updated as you proceed to build the file up.

This file will be invaluable to you when you come to write up your Business Plan.

> **Remember**, it is only yourself who will lose out if your business fails through lack of adequate research.

1 Motivation

 (a) Precisely why do you want to run your own firm?

 (b) What problems do you foresee in establishing it?

2 Product (or service)

 (a) Have you a marketable product or service? What, precisely, is it?

 (b) What actual evidence do you have that people really want (need) it?

 (c) What will be the level of demand that you expect to have to meet? What evidence exists for this view?

(d) Are there (will there be) competitors?

(e) What are the expansion prospects? On what are your assumptions based?

(f) Is further investigation needed? If so, into what?

(g) Will your customers come to you? If so, how do you propose attracting them? Or will you take the product to them? If so, how?

3 The firm's image,

(a) Have you a provisional name for your firm? What made you choose it? Is it one which will attract the customer?

(b) How do you propose to build up the 'image' of your product or service?

THE THIRD BIG QUESTION:
What about Premises?

One of the biggest problems which usually faces those wanting to start their own businesses is that of finding suitable premises. It is necessary to recognise this problem early in the planning process because if suitable premises are not available, then there is no way a successful business can be built up. Also, the cost of them is always a major item in the initial financing of a business, and this must form an important element in the consideration of a Business Plan.

EXISTING BUSINESSES

If you are buying an existing business, then it is likely that premises are already available and form part of the deal. However, caution must be exercised; it does not necessarily follow that the present site is the most suitable, even if it was once. It may be that the lease on the premises will shortly expire or that the landlord (if they are rented) has already given notice of an intention to increase the rent – and this could materially affect profit levels. There may have been (or shortly will be) a movement of population away from the present site, or there may be plans afoot for a new by-pass or similar development which will put the premises in a very disadvantaged position. It could well be that the premises are in a bad state of repair or have construction faults, and urgently need a considerable sum of money spending on them. After all, there must be some reason why the present owner wishes to sell, and the reason given may not be the real one.

The 'asking price' usually includes not only the premises, but also an amount for the stock and fittings, and for the goodwill. An intending purchaser should check carefully what, precisely, is being asked for what, and take

24 START YOUR OWN BUSINESS

professional advice regarding its fairness. Remember, goodwill can disappear overnight (and in any case will never be understated by a hopeful vendor), and the stock is often not worth the amount which is asked for it.

WORKING FROM HOME

Many who plan to start their own businesses 'from scratch' think of using the spare bedroom, or the garage, or the garden shed, for starters. Whether or not this can be done depends, to some extent, on the type of business which it is intended to run. Where it is possible, there are obvious advantages as regards saving of costs, ease and convenience, but such a solution may prove to be more attractive than practical.

First, there will almost certainly be, in the small print of the deeds or lease, '*restrictive covenants*' which prevent the use of the property for business purposes. In addition, planning permission is likely to be required, since the use of domestic premises for business purposes will involve what is known as a 'change of use'. If permission is granted, there could be a sharp increase in the rates payable on the property.

You may say '*Well, who is to know?*' and you may get away with it without anyone knowing, but if the type of business is one which is likely to cause any form of annoyance to the neighbours, then someone will soon know, and no doubt complain. And it can seriously undermine the success of a business to have to change premises shortly after starting.

Second, if you use your home for business purposes, and subsequently sell it, you may well find yourself liable for *capital gains tax*.

Third, even if there is sufficient space available at home to run the business properly at the moment, there may soon cease to be if it is successful and needs to expand – and *a move to new premises may seriously affect your customer support*.

Fourth, *it may be necessary to carry out conversions* to make the premises suitable, and to conform to the health and safety and the fire regulations.

Fifth, your present *insurance* almost certainly does not cover any activity associated with a business – in fact, the business may well invalidate the cover you already have on your domestic property.

Sixth and finally, *the social and psychological aspects* have to be considered. Running a business from home may well disrupt family life to a far greater extent than you first anticipate, and could well prove to be a serious cause of friction. Also, it is difficult – if not impossible – to develop at home the sense of discipline necessary to running a successful business. There will inevitably be interruptions from normal callers, phone calls, the washing-up to be finished, the dog to be taken out and the kids coming in from school demanding attention.

PREMISES: THE PRINCIPAL REQUIREMENTS

In assessing the suitability of premises, a number of factors have to be borne in mind. The design, size and layout are obviously important. It is difficult to know the best answers until you 'have lived with the business' for some while and you will almost certainly get it wrong in the first place. But this only emphasises the need for detailed investigation of needs and for careful planning beforehand, so that mistakes can be reduced to a minimum. Nothing undermines the quality of work more than not having sufficient space to do it in, together with difficulty in maintaining a proper flow of 'linked' operations.

Lighting and heating

Attention must be paid to correct lighting and heating. It will be impossible for workers to work efficiently if these are not right. The most desirable temperature for a room will depend very much on the type of activity which is to be performed there. Obviously, where physical activity is being undertaken, the optimum temperature will be lower than in a room where sedentary tasks are being undertaken. Even a room which is 'comfortable' for those performing clerical work may be regarded as 'hot' by typists.

Communications

Then there is the need for suitable telephone and postal facilities. Will one telephone be enough, or will several lines – and possibly a switchboard – be required? Will there be a need for any of the more sophisticated forms of communication, such as telex or facsimile transmission? All of these cost money, both to install and to operate, but proper communication with customers is essential if a business is to stand any chance of success.

Services

A further essential requirement, particularly for businesses employing a number of workers, is adequate 'service' facilities, such as toilets, wash and rest room accommodation, and – particularly for firms operating 'out of town' – food and refreshment facilities.

Special needs

The type of work with which a firm is concerned often means the premises have to meet special requirements. Presumably, you will know what these are from your specialist knowledge of the trade you intend to engage in, but such requirements as a three-phase electricity supply if machines are to be used, is a case in point. A further factor, if such machines are to be used, is whether the flooring is strong enough to take them – and to cope with the vibration which they will set up. In addition to all of these, it is essential that the fire regulations are satisfied – and these will vary considerably depending upon the type of work being undertaken. If you decide to go ahead with serious planning for a business, your local chief fire officer will be very pleased to give you help and advice.

Waste disposal

Satisfactory means for the disposal of waste will have to be looked into. This may be just a problem of quantity, but more difficult problems may arise if pollutants and toxic substances have to be disposed of, or if obnoxious fumes have to be dispersed. These are problems which are obviously very closely linked to the particular service which you intend to offer, and can only be considered in detail within that perspective. They are, however, the sort of questions which must be examined in detail when setting out the initial plans for your business.

Location

For many types of business, location is of crucial importance. This is particularly the case as regards retailing: a shop situated well away from its customers, and which is extremely inconvenient for them to get to, is hardly likely to be a success. Unfortunately, the answer is not as easy as that of simply meeting the customers' convenience, and usually has to be a balance between many competing considerations.

A manufacturing business, for example, may find it more cost effective to locate near the source of its raw materials than anywhere else. This is likely to be the case when the raw materials are far more expensive to transport than the finished product, or when the finished product has to be transported to widely separated parts of the country. The question of transport, in itself, is a consideration: how important is it for the business concerned to be near road, rail or air links?

Labour availability

Another important factor might be the availability of labour, particularly if the firm concerned is likely to be employing a relatively large workforce. Special problems are likely to arise where workers with special skills or experience will be needed: even today these can sometimes only be found in certain and restricted geographic areas, and it has often been found easier to take the work to the worker, than expect the workers to move to the work.

Car parking facilities

Car parking, in these modern times, is a far more important factor than it used to be. This is an important consideration, not only as regards employees and customers, but also as regards access to the premises for the off-loading of supplies. Most of us have seen, just within our own lifetimes, how the provision of a large car-park immediately adjacent to the premises has become, perhaps, the most vital consideration in deciding the location of supermarkets and, although most people wanting to start their own businesses will not be thinking in supermarket terms, it emphasises the importance of the consideration.

Competition

Some thought must be given to the question of whether it is better to set up a business near existing competitors, or well away from them. Both have advantages – and disadvantages. In retailing, in particular, certain streets in most towns become associated with particular types of trade; therefore, potential customers go to those areas in search for what they want. On the other hand, there will obviously be keen competition in such spots, and the new business may do better by setting up in an area where there are no others offering the same service. The reaction of existing residents may also have to be considered, particularly if the business concerned is likely to bring into the locality an 'undesirable' type of customer or will alter the 'character' of the area.

Development centre

Increasingly, opportunities are becoming available to obtain leases on units within special centres: these may be shopping precincts of one type or another, industrial and manufacturing locations, large office blocks, or 'nursery' units for new firms set up by local authorities at relatively cheap rents. These have many advantages which may include the provision of centralised services.

Social factors

Finally, if there is a choice of sites and there is little else between them, social factors may be important. Nearness, not only to transport routes but also to shopping centres, can be important if it is planned to employ married women, who have the problem of their homes to run as well as that of coming to work. A pleasant environment can also be important; no one likes working in a dirty, depressed – perhaps largely derelict – area with nothing but drab walls and grimy roofs to look out on, usually through mud-encrusted windows. And if potential employees are going to have to move house in order to work for you, then such things as availability of suitable housing, schools and leisure facilities become vital considerations.

TO BUY – OR NOT TO BUY?

Purchase

The outright purchase of premises can be expensive, but of course does have its advantages in terms of security of tenure and freedom to do (within certain constraints) what you want to with them. Before deciding on such a purchase, the intending buyer would be well advised to have a full and professional survey carried out, and to take advice regarding the fairness of the price being asked. It is also strongly advised that the actual conveyance of the property should be drawn up by a solicitor – preferably one experienced in the problems which arise in the buying and selling of industrial and commercial premises. He will be in a position to advise on restrictions regarding the use and possible development of the property – even the erection of signs and nameboards can involve legal difficulties. He will also enquire, if asked, into any planning and development plans for the area which might affect the new business. A close look must also be taken at the small print to make sure that there are no restrictions or obligations which will prove irksome.

It must be remembered, of course, that rates will be also payable on the premises purchased, and these have to be included in the costings attached to your initial business plan.

Leasing

Similar considerations apply to a lease except that there is the additional point regarding the length of time it has still to run. Remember, that at the end of the lease, the whole of the property – including any improvements or additions that may have been made to it – revert back to the owner of the freehold. The price of the lease should reflect the time left to run: when buying an existing lease, the purchaser should be careful that the vendor is not trying to recoup the costs for his own period of tenancy. The leaseholder may find that, in addition to the initial cost (the 'premium' as it is sometimes called), he is also responsible for the rates and even for redecoration and other costs at the end of the lease. This will be in addition to keeping the premises in a good condition throughout the period concerned.

A further point to check is whether there are any restrictions on subletting: if you have to wind up your business at a prematurely early date, you do not want to be saddled with premises of which you cannot make use.

Rentals

You may be able to obtain the property on a straightforward rental basis. This has the obvious advantage of low capital outlay, but a careful check should be made on security of tenure and on who is liable for the rates, repairs and redecoration. You should also find out whether there are any restrictions on the signs and fittings which you can erect.

The Landlord and Tenant Act gives some measure of protection to tenants, but nevertheless it can be a minefield for the unwary. Particular care is needed if you are subletting, since many of the rights under the act are granted principally to the occupier, not to the tenant. The act lays on the landlord the responsibility for initiating any action to end the lease or to raise the rent – even to evict the tenant at the end of the lease. The landlord has to serve upon the tenant a statutory notice giving twelve months' notice of an intention to end the lease or to raise the rent. The tenant, however, has a legal duty to reply within two months if he wishes the tenancy to continue or to be renewed – tenants lose their rights even if their reply is lost in the post. If there is likely to be a dispute, then application must be made to the court between two and four months after the issue of the notice by the landlord – and courts are obliged to apply these time limits absolutely rigidly.

Anyone likely to be affected by the Act should seek independent professional advice and guidance.

HELPLINE 1

Help in finding businesses for sale and premises. Try:

- Your local authority
  Most authorities have schemes under which various types of industrial premises can be made available to new businesses at sub-economic rents. Advice can usually be given on what else is available in the neighbourhood.

- Small Firms Service (now of the Department of Employment)
  Contact your local office (address in telephone directory) for advice.

- Rural Development Commission Business Service (formerly CoSIRA – Council for Small Industries in Rural Areas).
  For advice and help, contact your regional office (see telephone directory) or the head office: 141 Castle Street, Salisbury, Wilts SP1 3TP (0722 336255, Ext. 252).

- Dalton's Weekly
  Advertises businesses and premises on a national basis.

- Local newspapers and estate agents (see the *Yellow Pages*).

- Local business transfer agents (see *Yellow Pages* again).

TOWARDS YOUR BUSINESS PLAN

1   Premises already available

   (a)   Are they suitable?

   (b)   If you are using your own home, Have you checked out all the points raised in the section (pp.24-25)?

2   Premises still to be acquired

   (a)   What general nature and design required?

32 START YOUR OWN BUSINESS

    (b)   What general location?

    (c)   For what date are they likely to be required?

    (d)   Rent, purchase or lease?

    (e)   Are there likely to be problems of noise, pollution, waste? How can they be resolved?

    (f)   Any special requirements regarding services (e.g. water, electricity etc)?

    (g)   What storage facilities will be required?

    (h)   Any particular requirements regarding access?

    (i)   Any special provisions likely to be required regarding load-bearing, sound, ventilation, lighting?

    (j)   What problems in satisfying the requirements of the Health and Safety Act?

3   If, at this stage, you do not have any particular premises in mind, then draw up your 'ideal specification'. List, in detail, the principal features of the specification. When you do get as far as viewing several potential sites, check their features against your specification.

THE FOURTH BIG QUESTION:
Stocking Up

If you are to be successful in setting up your own business, one of the earliest – and indeed most important – management skills that you will have to learn is that of stock control. This will involve identifying what items of stock will be required both initially and subsequently once the business is in operation. Second, it will involve calculating the cost of 'stocking up' and of maintaining the stocks. This will involve finding out how much credit (if any) suppliers are willing to allow you. Third, it will involve deciding how quickly you will have to re-order stocks.

The stock items with which you will be concerned are not only those which you will be 'turning over' in the normal course of trade – such as raw materials in the case of a manufacturer or finished goods for re-sale in the case of a retailer – but also items such as stationery, spare parts, fuels and lubricants, and similar commodities necessary to keep the wheels of the firm turning.

STOCK CONTROL

Overstocking will mean tying up valuable working capital and storage space, both of which could be used more productively for other purposes; it will also mean risking loss from deterioration or obsolescence. *Understocking*, however, will mean the probability of running out of essential supplies at critical times, and this can seriously endanger the success of any business. Efficient stock control entails deciding on a very fine balance between the two, and involves:

(a) *ordering* the correct items in the correct quantities;

(b) *storing* them, once they have been delivered: and

(c) *recording* them in an efficient manner.

Ordering

The first step will be to estimate exactly what *items*, and what *quantities*, of stock will be needed. The second step will be to find suppliers who are both able and willing to supply the stock required. This may not be easy. For a number of reasons, a supplier may hesitate before taking on a new customer. He may have a 'sole agency' agreement with an existing trader in the area, or his production may already be fully committed. Also, suppliers are often not keen on extending credit to new traders until they have a successful 'track record' of profits and of settling bills on time. There is no easy answer to this problem: it means that the new trader should first of all see what credit terms – if any – he is able to negotiate, and to make appropriate allowances in his estimate of initial capital needed.

Considerable caution must be exercised. It is better to have more than one source of supply to prevent being held hostage through price increases or restrictions on supplies; and better credit terms may be obtained if the supplier concerned fears you might take your trade elsewhere. Again, it would be unwise to get tied to a supplier who is not reliable in terms of delivery dates or the quality of his goods, or to one who might be tempted to 'cut off' essential supplies just as the business is booming, particularly if he sees a chance of taking over the market you have created. Remember, there's no love lost in business.

Care must be taken that the supplier is willing to supply at a price which will enable a satisfactory profit to be made. The price of goods will usually, though not always, be quoted at what is expected to be their retail price to the consumer, but will be subject to an agreed rate of *trade discount*. The rate of this discount will be agreed between the new business man and the supplier, and may well vary depending upon credit status, size of order and how keen the supplier is to establish an outlet for his product in the area concerned. it is a discount which is *always* deductible, irrespective of when the account is paid and in this way differs from *cash discount* which is only allowed if the goods are paid for within a stipulated period of time. Cash discount – and also VAT (see p.106–108) – is calculated on the invoice price *less* the trade discount.

Trade journals and the *Yellow Pages* are useful sources of the names and addresses of potential suppliers. Advice from friends already in the trade can be invaluable, and the various advisory agencies (such as the Small Firms Service and the Rural Development Commission Business Service) will certainly do their best to help.

Many of the problems of stock supply are overcome if a franchise operation is in mind. The franchise operator will advise on stock levels, will arrange the supply of the goods concerned, and will usually be prepared to offer reasonable credit terms. The franchisee will, in all probability, be required under the franchise contract to obtain his supplies from the franchisor – this is fine except that the price of the goods may be higher than that ruling on the open market.

The difficulties may also be eased if one is buying an established business, but again caution must be exercised. Just because the vendor of the business had managed to 'knock along' for so many years, it does not mean to say that things have been organised in the most efficient manner. Also, the present suppliers may not be willing to continue to supply a new owner, and there may be far better sources available. Where businesses are sold with 'stock at valuation', be on your guard. The vendor will obviously be out for the best price he can get; much of the existing stock may be obsolete, and the price being asked for the rest may be too high. An intending purchaser would be well advised to obtain an independent valuation of it before agreeing a price.

Storing

Once the goods have been ordered, the next problems to be tackled are those connected with storing them. There are some obvious points which will have to be checked out. *Is the space available sufficiently large?* Remember that you will need working space to move, and sort out, the goods as well as to simply store them. *Is the shelving adequate?* And does it not only make the most effective use of the space available but enable a proper physical 'flow' of the various items through from initial receipt to ultimate issue? *Is the floor sufficiently strong to take the weight?* A large quantity of stock can be very heavy. *Is there satisfactory access?* The suppliers' vehicles will need to be able both to reach the premises concerned, and to have space to unload there. *Can the stores be issued without difficulty* but with a reasonable degree of security to the factory or shop? And, of course, *what major equipment will be needed*, such as forklift trucks, handling equipment, trolleys and the like?

Some more specialised questions will have to be considered, such as the need for *special provision for fragile or valuable stock*. Breakages and losses are an ongoing problem in any store, and the cost can be ruinous unless it is reduced to a minimum. *Refrigeration* may be needed for some items of stock, or *controlled conditions of humidity*. Other stock may need *special protection against damp and fire*. This means not only reducing fire risk by the proper and careful storage of flammable goods, but also the provision of adequate fire-fighting facilities should the unfortunate happen. Many stock items will be particularly dangerous if they ignite, and special provision will have to be made. If in any doubt at all on this matter, the advice of the local fire prevention officer should be sought at *the earliest possible opportunity*. The importance of doing this cannot be overemphasised.

Then there is the question of *security* – both the external threat of break-in and the internal threat from pilfering. Adequate lock-up arrangements, both of the premises as such, and of individual store-units will be needed. Security lighting and burglar alarms may have to be considered; there are a great variety of alarms now on the market. Considerable care must be taken before introducing measures – such as guard dogs and electrified fencing which could prove dangerous – if things go wrong. Take advice on this from a solicitor before making any decisions.

All police forces in the United Kingdom now have crime prevention officers whose duties include that of advising the public on all aspects of the security of their homes and their businesses. There is also a large number of security firms which will be prepared to give you a detailed analysis of a particular situation, and to make specific recommendations. This will, of course, cost money – but it is vital to remember that it will doubtless cost you far more if adequate security is not provided.

HELPLINE 2

For advice on the safety and security of stock and premises, contact:

- Local Fire Prevention Department
  Consult the Fire Prevention Officer; enquiries to local fire station.

- Crime Prevention Department
  The Crime Prevention Officer can be contacted through your local police station.

- Private security firms.
  See Yellow Pages *under (i) Security services (ii) Burglar alarms and security systems (iii) Safe and vault equipment.*

Stock records

The keeping of efficient stock records (or 'inventory control' as the Americans prefer to put it) is vital. Inadequate records mean that sooner or later the firm will run out of essential items, be grossly overstocked on others and encumbered with huge quantities of obsolete items. Also, it will have no adequate check on what is going missing and to prepare proper accounts will be an impossibility.

Put simply, the firm will be a living recipe for disaster.

A system *must* be devised which adequately records receipts, issues, and losses, and which alerts the storekeeper to the need for re-ordering as soon as it arises. It should also be possible to identify from such records those items which are not selling or being used.

In these days of cheap, highly efficient micros, a large range of off-the-shelf programs are available which will meet the needs of almost any firm. However, computer equipment can be expensive and it may be wise to wait until the firm is off the ground, and the precise problems are known, before investing.

In any case, whether computerised or not, it will be necessary to know what the main requirements of a system are, and the purpose of the documents involved. This is the only way to ensure that the system, whether or not computerised, meets your particular needs and requirements.

Stock records are based on a number of important documents which it is important to understand.

The first is a proper *order form*, preferably with the firm's printed letter-head. Although orders can be made by letter or even by phone, a supplier is not likely to be impressed by such an approach. Obviously, the order form should set out clearly exactly what goods are required, quoting catalogue or similar references, and should state any special requirements such as size or colour. Presumably, a check will already have been made on availability and delivery dates. The order forms should be sequentially numbered and a copy retained.

A *delivery note* should be attached to any consignment received. This should be checked against the order and the stock received recorded in an appropriately ruled *stock register* which will usually have a separate page for each stock item. In addition, the receipt should be recorded on an individual *bin card* which, as the name suggests, is usually attached to the actual storage unit.

Delivery notes only specify the quantities of stock being received. The cost will be stated on an *invoice* which may not arrive for a few days. The details of the invoice must obviously be checked carefully against the goods received register, and the cost recorded. This information will be vital in calculating (a) the cost of purchases for the trading period and (b) the value of closing stock, both of which are essential when computing profit. The invoices should be carefully filed under the name of the supplier concerned, and their total checked against the *statement* which will be received from the supplier shortly after the end of the month, and which will summarise the total owing.

Stock which is issued should be recorded in the *stores register* and on the appropriate bin card. It is vital that the

Figure 1 A simple form of stock register

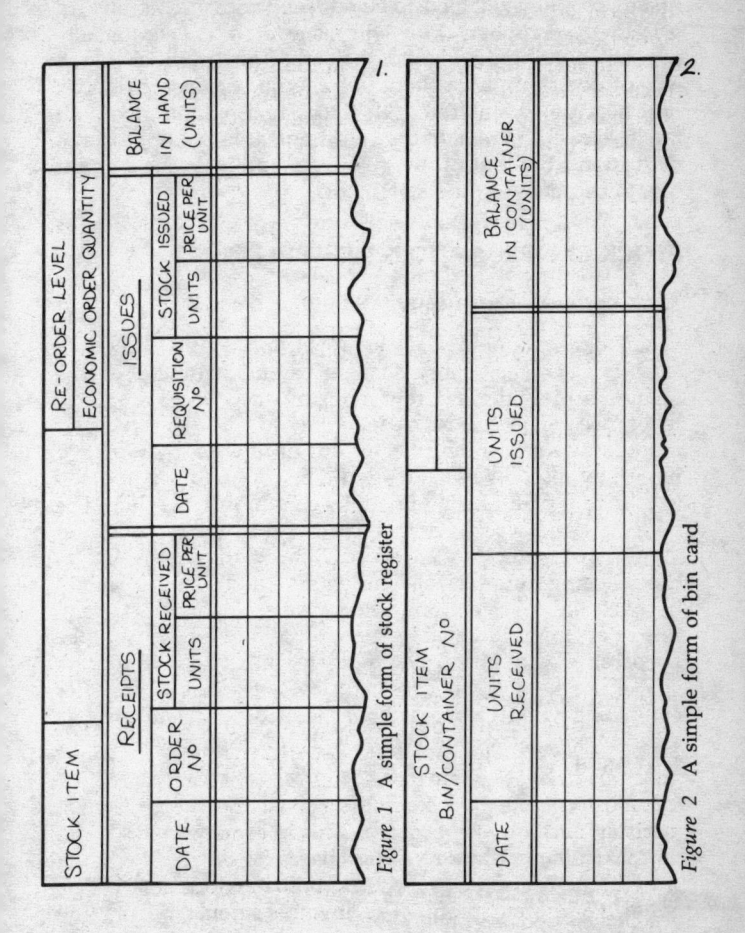

Figure 2 A simple form of bin card

balance still in hand of the item can be clearly seen and monitored.

It will sometimes be found that goods received are either faulty or damaged, or are not what was ordered in the first place. They will have to be returned with a *goods returned note* to the supplier, who will issue a *credit note* (usually printed in red to distinguish it clearly from an invoice). On receipt, the credit note should be checked against the goods returned record, entered in the stock register and filed with the invoices. The total of the credit notes should appear as a deduction from that of the invoices – and from the amount due to be paid – on the statement.

STOCK CONTROL AND A NEW BUSINESS

Stock control budgets

When starting a new business, it is important to draw up a *stock budget*. This consists of a careful estimate of the quantities of all the different items of stock which are likely to be needed in the foreseeable period – say the next six months or so. It should be set out on a week-by-week, or month-by-month basis and should be continuously updated as a 'rolling plan', i.e. additional weeks or months should be added as the weeks or the months go by. Obviously, it should try to anticipate any fluctuations in the need – such as those arising from seasonal variations – and columns should be available for recording what proves to be the 'actual' need, as this will enable more accurate forecasts to be prepared in the future. The budget will help to ensure that stocks are kept at an adequate level, provide a basis for estimating what capital will be needed, and will give an indication of how much this will be. From it, it will be possible to work out a time-plan for the actual ordering of goods.

Minimum stock re-order levels

Early in the life of the new firm – even if not before its birth – a *minimum stock level* will have to be decided for each stock-item: this is the level below which the stocks of the item concerned should never be allowed to drop before more is ordered. This figure refers to the amount of the item concerned which is likely to be needed by the firm until replacement supplies can be obtained – in other words, the

STOCKING UP 41

average daily consumption multiplied by the number of days delivery is likely to take.

The re-order levels should be clearly marked on the stock sheets and bin cards for the item concerned. It should have a built-in safety margin and may have to be adjusted in the light of changing circumstances. Care, however, must be

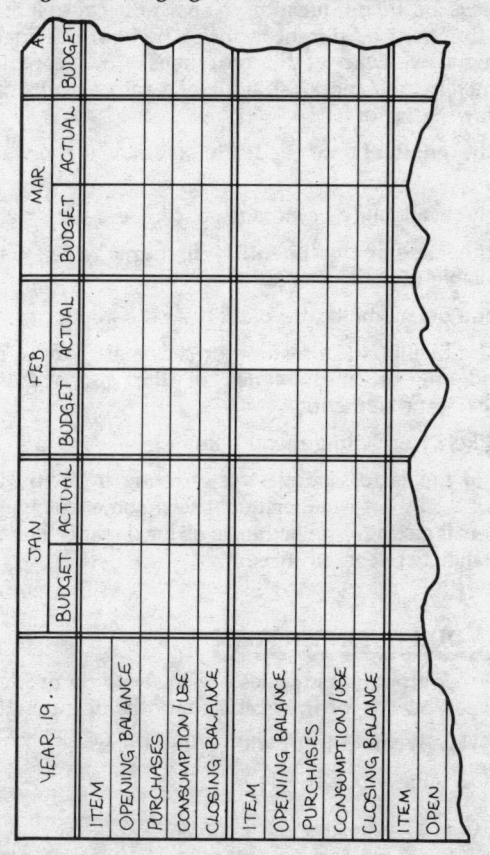

Figure 3 A simple stock control budget

taken not to be unnecessarily conservative – remember the danger of having too much capital tied up in idle stock.

Economic re-order quantity

When ordering from suppliers, *what is the best quantity to purchase?* This is a difficult question to answer because it is a balance of a number of different factors. The figure decided upon, which may well vary at different times of the year and with different circumstances, should take into account at least the following factors:

(a) the length of time needed to obtain delivery of an order;

(b) the availability of storage space;

(c) the value of any 'quantity' discounts which may be available in respect of large orders;

(d) the perishability or volatility of the goods;

(e) the likelihood of fashion or seasonal changes in demand, or of obsolescence of the goods from technical improvements;

(f) likely trends in general demand.

Some of the factors suggest re-ordering in relatively larger quantities, others smaller quantities; some involve a bit of crystal-ball gazing. The actual re-order quantity has to be a fine balance between all three.

TOWARDS YOUR BUSINESS PLAN

1. (a) Precisely what supplies are likely to be needed each week/month for the first six months of trading?

   (b) Who (i) can and (ii) will supply them?

   (c) On what terms?

2. (a) What do you consider to be your optimum stock levels of (i) raw materials and/or (ii) finished goods?

   (b) Calculate your minimum re-order quantities.

3   (a) What storage space do you anticipate you will require?

   (b) What fittings (shelves, bins, etc.) will be required?

   (c) What special facilities (e.g. refrigeration) will be required? What are they likely to cost?

   (d) Are special facilities likely to be required for packaging?

4   (a) Consider what documents (order forms, stock registers, etc.) you are going to need. Plan out draft copies of what you have in mind.

   (b) What is the anticipated cost of having them printed?

5   (a) What major items of equipment (e.g. forklift trucks) are likely to be needed?

   (b) What are you plans for acquiring these, and what is likely to be their cost?

6   (a) What fire precautions will need to be taken?

   (b) What security problems (internal and external) are likely to arise? Note your plans for coping with these.

THE FIFTH BIG QUESTION:
Gearing Up

In order to 'do something' with the stocks discussed in the last section, there will need to be the right equipment available. This will involve deciding (a) *what equipment will be needed*; and (b) *how much it will cost*.

WHAT EQUIPMENT?

The needs of firms will vary considerably and will be very specific to the particular type of business concerned. Some businesses will need to have little more than a stationery cupboard, filing cabinet and telephone (and maybe not even that). Most will need a range of furniture and furnishings: this may have to be both of the purely 'functional' type for the work area and of the 'image creating' type for the reception area. Some firms will need a range of heavy machinery, motor vehicles and sophisticated electronic equipment, and that sort of thing can be very expensive.

If a person 'knows' the industry he intends to enter, then he will already be aware of the type of equipment needed and the probable cost. If he is venturing out into a new field of which he is totally inexperienced, then he should start investigating the question very quickly indeed, for the costs and the various other problems involved may well mean that it is not feasible to go ahead. It will be a question of reading up and researching as much as possible about the product or service concerned, gleaning such information as is possible from those already in the field, and taking advice from suppliers and other specialists. The Rural Development Commission Business Service and the Small Firms Service will also probably be able to help.

A number of considerations arise with equipment which do not apply to trading stocks.

Permanence and cost

Equipment has two outstanding characteristics. First, once purchased it tends to remain a permanent 'fixed' asset of the firm concerned for some considerable while. Second, it can be very expensive and is unlikely to bring a quick cash return. If, therefore, wrong choices are made when the firm is being set up, big problems can result later.

Although equipment costs for some types of firm will be minimal, for others very heavy capital expenditure indeed will be involved. Serious consideration will have to be given to the various ways of financing it. In addition to other considerations, different forms of purchase carry different tax advantages and a careful comparison of these will be necessary.

Availability

A particular problem to be watched when planning a new firm is the supply date – in relation to the proposed start-up date – of equipment which has been ordered. It is obviously bad news to open the doors of a new firm – and then have to wait three months for the delivery of essential equipment. Some items, such as office equipment and standard tools, will be available 'off the shelf', probably both new and secondhand. Where the equipment is not immediately available, it may be necessary to obtain clear undertakings from the suppliers regarding the supply date and, if necessary, to write it into the contract as a condition of the purchase.

Maintenance and reliability

Equipment of the mechanical type will need regular servicing and maintenance. Servicing contracts will be worth considering, but care should be taken to ensure that the service which in fact is offered will be worth the annual servicing charge which is demanded. It *may*, but only may, be better to maintain and repair on a 'call-out when needed' basis.

Where items of equipment are so essential to the work of the firm that the whole operation grinds to a halt if there is a breakdown, it may well be worth considering having some sort of 'back-up' facility available. This may take the form of having alternative machines available, having an arrangement with another firm using identical equipment, or having a total support guarantee from the maintenance firm.

Operating skills needed

Many items of the more sophisticated type of equipment will need operators who have particular skills or have had appropriate training and experience. Such skills may already be available 'in family' as it were, or it may be possible to recruit as employees persons already trained. Also, suppliers of such equipment often provide minimal training – this may come free as part of the purchase price, or it may be an 'extra' – and sometimes a very expensive 'extra' it is too. If it is necessary to recruit someone and then send them for training, the costs – both financial and in terms of time – of this must be borne in mind when preparing the Business Plan. Also, the selection of the individual must be done with some care: no employer wants to go to the expense of training someone, then find that they leave the firm within a matter of weeks.

Operational planning

A number of operational factors will have to be considered at the initial planning stage. *Will the flooring be strong enough to accommodate the equipment?* If not, then either it will have to be strengthened, or an alternative location will have to be found. *Will there be a vibration or noise problem?* Vibration could affect other equipment in use by the firm. Both noise and vibration could lead to unpleasant working conditions for staff and might result in complaints from neighbours. *Will special services be required?* Examples include a three-phase electicity supply, washing and cooling facilities, fire-fighting and other safety devices. In addition, the layout of the equipment will have to be carefully planned to ensure the satisfactory 'flow' of work through the establishment and the reduction of workers' exertions – this 'fitting of the work to the worker' (as opposed to training the worker for the work) is known as *ergonomics* and it may be worth the while of intending business men – particularly those concerned with physical production – to look into its basic principles.

Expansion prospects

Business is about growth. Any person of spirit who starts a firm hopes that, no matter how small it is today, one day it will blossom forth into a major concern.

This means that, in choosing equipment, an eye must be kept on the expansion possibility. There are really three options available. The first is to *limit the purchase to equipment suitable for meeting the present foreseeable need*. This option will probably mean the smallest demand on the initial capital budget, but it may not be the cheapest in the long run if the business expands rapidly. The second option is *to choose equipment which would be capable of a greater output than that immediately foreseeable*. This will mean a heavier initial capital investment, but it will obviously be more economic – *if* the business does expand – than option one in the long run. The third option is to *buy equipment which has a satisfactory 'trade-in' option built into the purchase agreement*.

Safety

Finally, safety is a factor which must constantly be monitored. Some items of equipment, by their nature, have particularly dangerous characteristics. Where possible, guards and warning signs must be erected and every effort made to reduce the risk involved. Even equipment which in itself is basically harmless, can cause nasty injuries if not handled properly or maintained regularly. Electrical wiring, plugs and sockets, must also be inspected regularly. All staff must be made, and kept, fully aware of all potential hazards and of the procedures which *must* be followed to reduce the accident risk.

The Health and Safety at Work Act 1974 puts a very heavy duty indeed, not only on proprietors, but all those who have control of 'access to, and egress from' buildings to ensure safety. Hazards to the health and safety of employees and the public tend to be very much the same in small firms as in large, and the act does not distinguish between the sizes of the enterprises to which it applies. All employers and self-employed persons have the same responsibility to ensure as far as is reasonably practical that neither their own employees nor the public are at risk. Since small firms can face difficulties in meeting health and safety standards, the Health and Safety Commission and its Executive both pay particular attention to helping them to do so. When enforcing health and safety legislation, the main concern of inspectors must of course always be the health and safety of workers and the public, but they do not ignore the implications of their advice and requirements on the viability of the particular business they are dealing with.

HELPLINE 3

For advice and help concerning health and safety matters, contact:

1. *The Environmental Health Department of your local authority.*

   This department deals particularly in advice concerning pollution problems and waste disposal.

2. *Health and Safety Executive, (for local office, see telephone directory).*

   The Executive will be pleased to arrange for an inspector to call to give both general and specific advice. The following publications are available:

   - *Don't Wait until an Inspector Calls...*
   - *Writing a Safety Policy Statement. Advice to Employers.*
   - *500 Dead.*
   - *Health and Safety in Small Clothing Factories.*
   - *Essentials of Health and Safety at Work. This has been written specifically for those setting up a new firm or managing a small work unit and gives practical advice on identifying work hazards, assessing the risks to employees and others, and planning the action needed to reduce or eliminate risks.*

Inspectors are always pleased to visit new firms. Their advice regularly covers:

- the legal requirements which apply to the particular business;

- practical advice on what needs to be done to ensure the health and safety both of the employees and of non-employees;

- how to assess risks and devise the most appropriate and cost effective control measures;

- the availability of published and other sources of information;

- the legal requirements and any standards which might apply to the articles and substances produced by the firm.

Intending business men should not hesitate to take the advice of the Health and Safety Executive. It will be given freely and gladly. But, remember the inspectorate can close premises at a moment's notice if it is felt that essential safety obligations are being ignored.

WHAT ABOUT COMPUTERS?

One item of equipment which most firms can use to advantage these days is a computer, and their cost is now so reasonable that businesses can usually be planned around them from the start – in fact, there are many advantages in doing so. However, it is crucial that the right machine is used, in the right place, at the right time and for the right function.

The three main uses that a computer is likely to be put to are wordprocessing, accounting and stock control. It does not need a lot of imagination to see that these uses are not necessarily independent, and for some firms a fully integrated system, which will automatically link up these elements, will be the best way forward.

For most firms just starting up, microcomputers are quite sufficient for these routine tasks. The options available are either to buy a whole system, including the machines (the hardware) and the programs (the software) from a computer supplier, or to choose your own software from one of the many software packages available – taking care, of course, that it is suitable for your needs – and to buy an appropriate machine from a high street dealer. If in doubt about what to buy, try to find out if there is a local ITEC (Information Technology Centre) – they will talk through your needs with you and offer some advice.

To use any of today's packages, it is not necessary to know anything about computers or even how to type. What is necessary is an enquiring mind, with a desire to look beyond your immediate needs, an ability to read and make reference to a manual and, ideally, good back up from a supplier or another user, to point you in the right direction if you come up against a stumbling block. Remember, computers won't be broken by normal use, but good housekeeping is essential if they are to be used efficiently.

When exploring the systems available on the market, ensure that you have a list of questions to which you need to know the answer and some idea of the number of clients or components that you are likely to be dealing with. Computer firms are very willing to offer advice on how their system will tackle the tasks they think your firm needs to perform. What is sometimes difficult is for the firm to explain how the system will tackle the tasks you think your firm will need to perform.

There is no substitute for talking with firms which currently use a system you are considering. Any computer supplier who has confidence in his own product will be happy to refer you to such a firm. Take advantage of the offer, leave plenty of time for the visit and take your list of questions along. Many of these will be answered in the course of a demonstration and general discussion, but it's worth checking the list at the end to see if there are any outstanding questions. If that firm cannot answer them, then perhaps another firm or the supplier can. If they can't, then it may be worth looking at another system.

It is as well to remember that only one person can

operate a keyboard at any time, so if there is likely to be a need for various people to access the machine, a networked system is worth looking at. This will provide, at a cost, more than one access point, but still enable the firm to operate an integrated system.

For some businesses, even those for which a computer is not necessary, a wordprocessing machine may be preferable to the traditional typewriter, and often at no greater cost. The only drawback is that it is more difficult to complete preprinted forms on a wordprocessor than on a typewriter, but there are many advantages to outweigh this.

Small, very effective, inexpensive computers for wordprocessing exist, which can easily be used by inexperienced operatives and can perform routine typing work as well as updating lists and making total and selective mail shots. There are commercial accounting packages that can be used on these machines, but they are primarily wordprocessors.

Such machines produce good quality output, either with a letter quality 'daisy wheel' printer, or near letter quality 'dot matrix' printer. The advantages of the first are that the print is indistinguishable from that of a typewriter, of the second that a variety of typestyles can be produced within any one document. If a dot-matrix printer is used with a carbon ribbon, then there is very little difference to choose between the quality of the output from a daisy wheel or a dot-matrix printer.

Computers are like any machine – they tend to find their own work and their use usually expands far beyond what was originally intended. Many systems are capable of being 'upgraded', in terms of additional memory, input stations or printers, but always at a cost. Before you invest in one, make sure you know what it can do at the start, what it's promised it can do if required, and at what cost, and what you can expect in the way of training and backup in the event of failure.

THE FINANCIAL ASPECT

There is a wide range of individual financial schemes available from the various finance companies to assist with the purchase of capital equipment: each has its advantages, each its disadvantages, and each its 'gimmick'. Since major sums of capital expenditure may well be involved, the confusing array of options on offer should be carefully researched. It would be impossible in a short book to give a complete breakdown of all the possibilities; however, most are variations on one of three main schemes.

Outright purchase

This is obviously the simplest method of all. It means that there is no 'drag' on profits later, and no interest payments to be met. On the other hand, it entails laying out a very heavy capital sum right at the start – more than a new business may be able to afford. Capital allowances will be claimable which will reduce the burden of tax on profits. At the time of writing, the capital allowance on a new asset is 25% of its price set against profits in the year of purchase. In addition, the VAT may in most cases be reclaimed by registered firms – the main exception is the purchase of cars.

Lease

Leasing means, simply, renting. The asset does not become the property of the firm taking the lease, though some leasing arrangements include a 'rebate' provision under which some reduction of the normal purchase price can be obtained if at some stage during the leasing it is decided to change to outright purchase. The advantage of leasing is that it involves the minimum in terms of immediate capital outlay, and the periodic lease payments coincide with the working life of the asset. The lease is regarded as a 'revenue expense': this means that it is deductible from income when calculating profit. Tax relief is given on the full lease charge. Also, VAT is usually reclaimable. There is, of course, no right to capital allowances.

Lease-purchase and hire-purchase

There is a particularly wide variety of lease-purchase schemes on the market. They are an attempt to combine the advantages of both leasing and purchase. Payments are spread over an agreed period – usually shorter than normal leasing periods – and technically the asset is leased until the final payment, when it may be purchased for a purely nominal amount. Obviously, the cost is greater than that under simple leasing. For taxation purposes, the asset is assumed to be purchased immediately, and the normal capital allowances are given on the purchase price of the asset as such. The periodic payments made under a lease-purchase agreement will involve an interest element, and this amount can be set against profits as a revenue expense, thus attracting normal tax relief. Subject to the usual restrictions and exceptions, VAT will be reclaimable.

For all practical purposes at this stage, hire-purchase can be regarded as similar to lease-purchase, though the comparative interest rates and the 'small type' of the agreement should be watched. The goods are, strictly, on hire until the last instalment, when the transfer of legal ownership takes place. As with lease purchase, for accounting and tax purposes the instalments less the interest element are regarded as instalments on the capital cost, not as payments for hire which is what they are in law.

TOWARDS YOUR BUSINESS PLAN

1   The equipment

    (a)   What equipment will your firm need?

    (b)   Who can supply it?

    (c)   At what price?

    (d)   What will be the delivery period?

2   Finance

    (a)   Prepare a comparison of the costs under alternative financing arrangements.

    (b)   What other pros and cons, as far as your business will be concerned, apply to the alternative financing methods?

    (c)   Make a preliminary decision on the best financing arrangement for you.

54 START YOUR OWN BUSINESS

3 Operation

(a) What special skills will be needed to operate the equipment?

(b) Are they available?

(c) Will training be needed? What are your plans to obtain it?

4 Health and safety

(a) What health and safety risks exist to:
   (i) employees
   (ii) public?

(b) How do you intend to cope with these?

(c) Have you been in touch with:
   (i) the Local Authority
   (ii) the Health and Safety Executive?
   If not, when will be a suitable time to make an approach?

THE SIXTH BIG QUESTION:
Staffing up

We have looked at the product, the premises, the stock and the equipment. Now we must look at the staffing requirement.

It may be possible, at least in the early stages of a business, for the owner to do all the work himself. Even this, however, should be the result of a considered decision based on a proper assessment of the staffing needs. For most firms, later if not sooner, employees will have to be recruited – and a mistake in the exercise can be expensive.

In one sense, the staffing problem is a unique one. In all of the other problems which a business owner has to face, only inanimate objects like machines and money and tins on shelves are involved. The only person who suffers if he makes a mess of it is himself. But when it comes to staffing, he is dealing with human beings – and with their lives and their future. Not, in other words, something to be tampered with lightly or irresponsibly.

The main questions which arise are:

(a) *when* should someone be recruited;

(b) *who* should be recruited;

(c) *how* should the recruit be chosen; and

(d) *what* are the law's demands?

ESTIMATING STAFFING NEEDS

An important task in the early plans for a business is to look closely at the jobs which will need doing and to make as fair an assessment as is possible of the *amount* of the work which will need doing, the *time* when it will have to be done, and the *nature* of the work involved.

56 START YOUR OWN BUSINESS

The first question involves deciding how many staff will be required. It will probably be very difficult to estimate the workload before the business has started operating, and the first concern will be to meet the likely immediate, short-term need. Once the dust has settled and it can be seen exactly what the level of demand for the firm's services is likely to be, it will obviously be much easier to make an accurate appraisal of the firm's needs. It will help greatly in this initial period if the family can be pressed into service, or if persons are available who would be willing to work on a part-time or temporary basis. However, care must be taken not to undermine the quality of the firm's service through the employment of staff not wholly committed to the business and its work.

The second question involves an estimate of how quickly (or slowly) the firm is likely to expand. If sufficient staff have been recruited for immediate needs, then plans for the longer term future can be allowed to pend for a while – but not too long as the process of recruitment, selection and training can take quite a while and the firm that wins is the one that has the right staff in post at the right time.

The third question involves a careful analysis of the technical skills and personal qualities which may be required. A decision will have to be taken whether to recruit someone ready-trained, or whether the firm will be prepared (and able) to train whoever is appointed. The relative costs involved will have to be borne in mind when preparing the cash flow forecasts (see pp.110-113). In addition to formal training in the necessary skills for the job, all new employees may need a short induction and training programme to acquaint them with the methods and philosophy of the new firm. This will be particularly important for young recruits to whom the world of work may be a very strange place. If the new firm comes under the umbrella of an industrial training board (ITB), advice and help with training will be available. Most ITBs give grants to firms which provide training, recouping the cost by a levy on all firms within the industry – or, at least, the larger firms. Small firms may exempt. A group training association may exist for smaller firms, and the MSC may also be able to provide help through its direct training services.

STAFFING UP 57

SOURCES OF RECRUITMENT

Recruiting the *right person for the right job* is the key to a successful personnel policy. Mistakes can be very expensive – even disastrous. Much of the secret is knowing where to look in the first place, and where to look will depend largely on the sort of person being sought.

The first source is personal knowledge: you may already know just the right person for the job and you will be able to 'head-hunt' him or her. The second source is the careers service and job centre or – for higher level appointments – the professional and executive recruitment register. Advertisements can be placed in the corner shop (suitably particularly for part-time unskilled staff), in the local or national press, or in trade journals for the more specialised staff. Then there are the private recruitment agencies – but be careful of the cost to these. Finally, do not ignore your local schools and colleges – the careers staff there will be delighted to help you.

Advertisements should be worded carefully, and the main points which should be included are set out below. Some employers may prefer not to mention some of the points – fine, but they should not complain if they are swamped with applications from unsuitable persons.

In advertising for staff – and indeed in promotions and dismissals subsequently – you must be careful not to show discrimination, as regards either sex or race. All posts, with only a very few limited exceptions, must be equally open to everyone.

From the applications received, a short list of persons who appear worth interviewing should be drawn up. People who have not conducted interviews before tend to find interviewing difficult – and are usually as nervous about it as those who are being interviewed. Much has been written about the art of interviewing; it is certainly a skill which will develop with time and experience. Nevertheless, some simple guidelines may help.

First, *make sure you have read the application thoroughly before the interview*, noting any points you may want to take further. It is time-wasting to ask questions the answers to which are already in the application (unless, of course, this is done deliberately to set the applicat at ease or to give him a

ADVERTISING FOR THE RIGHT PERSON

Check that the advert includes

1. Job title
2. Outline description of duties
3. Age and experience required
4. Location of the job
5. Pay scale (statement of any extras – eg. transport or lunch vouchers
6. How to apply – in person? by phone? by form? in writing (hand or typewritten)?
7. Whether further details are available, or contact for further information
8. Closing date for applications
9. Names, addresses and positions of persons to whom reference can be made
10. Name and address of firm (or, alternatively, box number) to which applications should be addressed.

chance to expand the information). Second, *ensure that the applicant is met and properly welcomed on arrival, and shown where to wait*. It is always helpful if a short tour or talk about the firm can be given by yourself or by an assistant. Third, *invite the applicant into the interview room courteously*, introducing yourself and anyone else in the room whilst introducing the candidate. Make sure you invite the applicant to sit down! Fifth, *ask, the candidate a few general questions* designed to break the ice and put him or her at ease. *Follow these up with more specific questions* designed to ascertain the person's suitability for the job from the point of view of qualifications, experience, motivation and ambitions. Remember, good questions will seldom occur to you on the spur of the moment and they should be carefully planned out beforehand in a structured sequence – after all, you can always depart from your plan if you wish. 'Trick' and aggressive type questions should be avoided (you have to be really skilled before you can use these and even then their value might be questioned) but this is not to say that questions should not be designed to 'check back' on previous questions and their answers. The formulation of questions which will really bring out what you wish to know about a candidate is very difficult, and will require much careful thought and preparation beforehand – though it is a skill you will get better at with more experience. Sixth, *the candidate should be invited to raise any points, and to ask any further questions*, which he or she wishes. Finally, unless a decision can be given immediately, *the candidate should be informed of the arrangements for informing him or her of the result* – whether, for example, a decision will be announced at the conclusion of the interviews of all the applicants present, or whether (and when) they will be informed by post.

CONDITIONS OF EMPLOYMENT

All full-time (i.e. those working 16 hours a week or more) employees are now entitled to a written contract of employment within thirteen weeks of their appointment. This is, legally, more of a statement of the terms and conditions, rather than the contract itself – the contract exists from the time your offer, as an employer, has been accepted by the employee even though nothing has been committed to writing. What should go into the written statement is set out below.

With a few exceptions, there are now no minimum wage scales which must be paid, but there *must* be equal pay for men and women undertaking 'like work'. Also, employees are entitled to a statement with their pay packets giving details of gross wage, all deductions, and net wage. The employer is responsible for deducting national insurance contributions and PAYE tax. These deductions, together with the employer's own contribution to his workers' national insurance must be paid to the local collector of taxes.

Certain occupations, e.g. shop assistants and road transport drivers, and certain groups of employees, e.g. those under 18, are subject to restrictions on the maximum

Make certain the following points are covered:

1. The full job title
2. Full details regarding pay and pay scale
3. Details of holiday entitlements
4. Pension scheme details (if any)
5. Statement whether a contracting-out certificate is in force which would apply to the employee
6. A precise statement of hours of work
7. Details of sick pay entitlements
8. Notice required from both sides for termination of employment
9. Disciplinary rules and procedures
10. Person or body to whom the employee can appeal if dissatisfied with any disciplinary action

hours they can be required to work. The Health and Safety Executive (see Helpline 3, p.48) will advise on current regulations regarding particular employments.

A woman employee has a right to attend an antenatal clinic and has certain rights regarding maternity pay and leave, and to return to work after delivery of her child. The current regulations can be obtained from the Department of Employment.

The law does not like clauses in an employment contract which limit the right of an employee to work after leaving a particular job, and will not usually enforce them even if the employee has previously agreed to them. The onus is on the employer to show that the restrictions are necessary – such, for example, to prevent advantage being taken of confidential lists of customers or of secret industrial processes acquired during employment. In addition, the employer must show that the restriction is reasonable as regards (a) the functions and skills restricted, (b) the geographic area over which the restriction applies, and (c) the time period for which it will last. (This is, of course, in sharp contrast with the position regarding such clauses in contracts for the sale and purchase of a business as a going concern, where the law assumes the restriction is necessary and reasonable and the onus is on the purchaser to show that they are not).

Care must be taken to ensure that premises are safe and that there is proper protection from dangerous machinery, chemicals and fumes. The minimum health and safety requirements vary from industry to industry, and again the advice of the Health and Safety Executive should be sought.

New firms are likely to be more concerned with recruiting staff rather than getting rid of them. However, hard times may come unexpectedly, and it may be necessary to put on to short time, or even make them redundant. Complicated provisions now exist to safeguard the interests of workers in these situations and the advice of the Department of Employment should be sought at as early a stage as possible.

Employment may be terminated by either side giving the required period of notice. The employer may, if he wishes, pay wages in lieu of notice whilst the employee, if he has been given notice, is free to leave without penalty immediately if and when he has the chance of another job. An employee is entitled, on request, to a written statement of reasons if he has been dismissed and is entitled to have his side of the story heard. Only in exceptional circumstances can an employee be 'summarily dismissed' – that is, dismissed without notice. Theft or serious assault at the workplace could be examples.

Workers often request a testimonial or reference on leaving employment. There is no obligation upon an employer to give one, though it may well be thought unreasonable if he refuses since a wrong interpretation may well be put on such an action. If one is given, there is no obligation upon the employer to include any particular comment or statement – but what is said, must be true to the best of the knowledge of the employer. References are, however, protected in law by what is known as *qualified privilege*, which means that the employer giving a bad reference would only be liable if it could be shown that he had deliberately made untrue statements, or made them recklessly without belief in their truth. Employers giving references may, however, find themselves liable to the new employer. This could arise, for example, if it was known that the new employer was likely to rely on a statement of honesty in the reference, and this was given knowing the employee to be dishonest. No liability would arise however, by simply omitting reference to it.

There is one further way in which employers must have a close regard for the law. If personal information about individuals is kept on a computer – such, for instance, as a staff or personel record – then the employer will probably be required to register under the Data Protection Act 1984. Registration would also be required where, for example, personal information and credit status information is recorded regarding customers.

Any individual whose personal details are included on the computer file is entitled, on request, to have a print-out of the information which has been recorded about him. The act does not apply where information is kept manually. A number of guidelines to the act are available from the Data Protection Registrar.

Since fines for offences under the act are unlimited, it would be wise for any employer likely to be affected to contact the Data Protection Office, Springfield House, Water Lane, Wilmslow, Cheshire SK9 5A (0625 535777) at the earliest opportunity to make further enquiries.

TOWARDS YOUR BUSINESS PLAN

1   Plan a schedule of the staff which will be needed:

    (a)   in the short term

    (b)   in the long term.

2   Identify:

    (a)   what special skills or abilities each of the workers will need

    (b)   the possible sources from which each can be recruited

    (c)   the training which each will/may require

(d) how that training can be obtained.

3 Consider the interviewing and selection techniques you will need to employ.

4 Estimate the possible costs of:

(a) advertising and interviewing (out-of-pocket expenses are normally paid to those interviewed)

(b) training.

5 Estimate the probable wage cost (including employer's national insurance contributions, possible sick pay, holiday pay, etc.).

6 Decide what welfare facilities (e.g. canteen, transport, health) will be needed and estimate their cost.

7 Consider how you will develop good industrial relations within your firm and prepare a statement of practices which you can discuss with the appropriate trade unions. Prepare also a statement of disciplinary procedures.

8 Prepare an outline of the written statement of the conditions of employment which you will give to each member of your staff.

Be prepared to link the data you prepare here with that prepared in other sections – there will obviously be some overlap in the information required under different heads.

THE SEVENTH BIG QUESTION:
What Legal Format?

When you start your business, you will have to decide what legal form it should take – and as it (hopefully) grows, you may have to consider whether its form should be changed to meet new demands.

There are three main forms of organisation which can be considered: sole proprietorships, partnerships and companies. A variation of these is workers' co-operatives. Each form has its advantages, each its disadvantages. Careful thought must be given, well before you intend to start operating, as to which form you are going to adopt.

SOLE PROPRIETORSHIPS

Most businesses start their life as either sole proprietorships or partnerships. A *sole proprietorship* is (as the name suggests) a firm which is wholly owned by one person. Indeed, such firms are often referred to as 'one-man' businesses, but this is misleading as more than one person may be employed within the firm concerned.

One of the reasons why a sole proprietorship is an attractive proposition in a start-up situation is that it is the simplest form of business undertaking. But there are other advantages.

One is that profits do not have to be shared. Another is that decisions can be taken 'on the spot' without having to obtain the agreement of a partner or board of directors. Also, the legal formalities are minimal and are limited to letting the Inland Revenue and the Department of Health and Social Security know what is intended. If business is to be carried on under a 'trade name', then the proprietor must disclose his actual name on the firm's bills and letterheads. Apart from these minimal restrictions, forming a sole proprietorship is both cheap and easy.

WHAT LEGAL FORMAT? 65

There are, however, some disadvantages. One is the fact that the firm's capital will be limited to that which the sole proprietor can raise himself, either from his private resources or by way of loan – which brings up the problem of how much security he can offer. It also means that the ideas floating around within the firm are usually just his own – he cannot 'bounce them off' equally committed partners, or pick up ideas from them. It means, also, that the owner has no one to share the firm's problems with, which means that the stress factor can be very high indeed. And one of the biggest snags is that the owner has full liability for the debts of the firm: even his own private possessions, which are nothing whatsoever to do with the firm as such, can be seized in settlement of the business's debts.

A sole proprietor has to pay normal income tax on his firm's profits. However, the system is a little different from that which applies to ordinary employees – the tax payable for a particular year will normally be based on the profits made by the firm in the *preceding* financial year. Special provisions apply when the firm first commences trading, and when it ceases: these are too complicated to explain here, and advice should be sought from an accountant or a solicitor. The Inland Revenue issue a useful booklet called *Starting a Business* (IR28) This is well worth reading and can be obtained on request from your local tax office.

A sole proprietor has to pay national insurance contributions at the flat rate class 2 rate, and may also have to pay a class 4 contribution. The legal position is complicated, and a person intending to set up business should obtain the advice of his local DHSS office at an early date – certainly before the actual commencement of business. A number of pamphlets are available which help to explain the position.

All employers are of course, responsible for deducting income tax and national insurance from the wages paid to their employees, and for paying these deductions over to government. The Inland Revenue issue a number of pamphlets and guides which attempt to explain the procedures which have to be followed, but it is a complicated routine and, unless you know what you are doing, the advice and help of someone who does should be sought.

Your employees will not thank you if you get their tax affairs in a mess.

Apart from the normal State 'old-age' pension, there is no in-built superannuation scheme available to sole proprietors. If you are starting your own business, and you want to look forward to retiring from it on a nice, comfortable pension, then you must obviously be prepared to make provision for it. All life assurance companies have their pet schemes for this, and none of them will be slow in telling you how suitable their particular plan is for you. A good idea would be to take the advice of an independent insurance broker specialising in the pensions field, who is 'authorised' to give such advice under the Financial Services Act. The British Insurance and Investment Brokers Association (BIIBA) of 14 Bevis Marks, London EC3A 7NT (01 626 9676) will be pleased to supply a list of approved professional brokers practising in your area.

PARTNERSHIPS

Partnerships consist of firms which have at least two joint proprietors. Unlike sole proprietorships, partnerships are subject to a specific law – i.e. the Partnership Act of 1890. This Act, however, only lays down a bare framework. Those intending to enter into this type of business relationship would be well advised to draw up – or preferably have drawn up by a solicitor – a carefully thought-out partnership agreement. Some of the more important clauses which should go into such an agreement are:

- Capital to be contributed by each partner
- Interest (if any) to be allowed to partners on capital
- Procedure for partners making loans to the partnership
- Interest (if any) payable to partners on loans
- Specific statement of the duties and responsibilities of each partner

WHAT LEGAL FORMAT? 67

- Salaries (if any) to be paid to partners
- Ratio in which profits and losses are to be divided between partners
- Procedure for drawings by partners
- Interest (if any) to be charged on drawings
- Involvement of each partner in the management and decision-making processes
- Accounting provisions and rights of partners to inspect the books
- Procedure on the death, retirement or withdrawal of partners, including the calculation of goodwill and the procedure for paying out to the partner or his estate his share of the partnership assets
- Procedure in the event of sickness or incapacity of a partner
- Rules regarding conduct which might be regarded as against the interests of the partnership
- Restraints on undertaking work which would compete with the partnership if a partner withdraws
- Procedure to be followed regarding the admission of a new partner, including the calculation and payment of goodwill
- Rules and procedure to be followed in the event of the dissolution of the partnership, including the division of surpluses and deficits on the winding up
- Procedure – arbitration or otherwise – for resolving disputes between the partners.

In the absence of a clear partnership agreement – *and only in its absence* – the Act lays down that no interest should be allowed on partners' capitals (no matter by how much the amount put into the firm by the partners may differ), no salary should be payable (irrespective of how much more work one partner may do compared with the others), that interest on loans – as opposed to capital – to the partnership should be at 5% (easy to see that the act is an old one!) and that profits – or losses – should be divided among the partners equally.

The advantage of forming a partnership is that it brings an extra person into sharing the burden of running the business – often one who can contribute special skills, knowledge or contacts and who can provide extra capital.

But there are some major snags. Partners, when it comes to it, may not be willing to pull their weight, and this can increase the stress and worry of running the business instead of decreasing it. It also means the profits have to be divided as many ways as there are partners. More particularly each partner remains individually and personally liable to creditors for the full amount of the firm's debts – though if any one partner pays them, he is entitled to proceed against the others for their share. Each partner is also liable for any civil wrongs (known in law as *torts*) committed by himself, by any other partner, or by any of the employees, within the scope of the partnership business. Such a liability could arise, for example, from injury to a pedestrian through the negligent driving of a van by an employee of the firm. It is in this unlimited liability of each individual partner for the whole of the debts of the firm that there lies the biggest disadvantage of this particular form of business organisation.

It is possible to form what is known as a 'limited' partnership under an Act passed in 1907. This enables some partners to have their liability for the debts of the firm limited. However, such partners are not allowed to take any part in the running or management of the firm whatsoever. In addition, every limited partnership must have at least one 'general' partner whose liability remains unlimited. This, together with the development shortly after the Act was introduced of the idea of a 'private' company – which can be formed easily and cheaply, and which gives limited liability to all – has meant that very few limited partnerships have been formed.

Partners are subject to normal income tax in the same

way as sole proprietors. The full profits will count as income of the partners, who will each be responsible for claiming their individual personal allowances. Each partner is also liable for national insurance as a self-employed person.

If you decide on a partnership, choose your partners with caution. Remember, you are going to be working with them and alongside them for a very long time. A chap who is a good drinking mate in the pub at night will not necessarily make a good business partner. Partners are (fairly) easily acquired, but they can be very difficult indeed to get rid of.

COMPANIES

Companies are rigidly controlled by law, namely the Companies Act 1985 and subsequent legislation. The act has to be strictly complied with, and contraventions of it can carry heavy fines and terms of imprisonment. It is a form of organisation designed primarily for larger companies, though the limitation on the liability of members for the debts of the company make the idea attractive to medium and even small-sized firms. The pros and cons of forming a company are discussed in the next section.

WORKERS' CO-OPERATIVES

Despite the early success of *retail* co-operatives, there has been no marked development of workers' co-operatives in this country although there has been some quickening of interest just over the past few years. This has stemmed, in some cases, from threats of close-down of existing industry and, in other cases, from unemployed workers getting together and deciding to 'do their own thing'.

Co-operatives vary in form and character, but the main idea behind most of them is that the management, objectives and use of assets should be controlled by the workforce, with decisions being made by democratic vote of all involved. Ideally, everyone has an equal but limited financial investment and profits are distributed equally to all.

Most business formats are suitable for particular types or size of enterprise; co-operatives appear to be no exception. They have worked reasonably well where they

HELPLINE 4

Help for co-operatives

Co-operative Advisory Group
Antonia House, 262 Holloway Road, London N7 6NE
(01 609 7017/8)
Provides business advice services, various forms of practical assistance and training courses.

The Co-operative Bank
1 Balloon Street, Manchester M60 4EP (061 832 3456)

The Co-operative College
Stanford Hall, East Leake, Loughborough, Leics LE12 5QR (050 982 2333)
Provides various courses of training, residential and by correspondence, for those interested in co-operatives.

The Co-operative Development Agency
Broadmead House, 21 Panton Street, London SW1Y 4DR (01 839 2988)
Promotes, trains, advises. Makes recommendations to government and carries out research and acts as forum for the co-operative movement. Sponsors co-operatives and produces model rules and constitutions on a custom fit basis.

The Co-operative Union Ltd
Holyoake House, Hanover Street, Manchester M60 0AS
(061 832 4300)
Main organiser, adviser and spokesperson for the consumer co-operative movement in the UK; provides a wide range of services to its member societies, offers help and advice with registration under the Industrial and Provident Societies Acts for certain types of new co-operatives.

Industrial Common Ownership Finance Ltd
1 St Giles Street, Northampton NN1 1SA (064 37563)
Provides loan finance to new and expanding workers' co-operatives normally over a five-year period.

Industrial Common Ownership Movement
Vassalli House, 20 Central Road, Leeds LS1 6DE (0532 461737)
Provides assistance with registration, model rules, legal problems.

have involved a few committed and highly motivated individuals prepared to work together. They have shown themselves capable of working at lower levels of profitability and growth, and therefore better able to cope with crises and lean periods than purely commercial organisations. They also enjoy support from the major political parties.

Difficulties, however, have tended to arise when co-operatives have wished to expand beyond a limited base, particularly where this might mean introducing new members who may not be committed to the co-operative philosophy. Friction has sometimes developed where the work load has been unequal and the structure of the co-operative has prevented this from being adequately recompensed. Also, the system of controlling everything by a majority vote based upon a broad-based participation has sometimes led co-operatives along avenues which have not been the most desirable from a professional management point of view.

Legally, workers' co-operatives may exist as partnerships (in which case liability is unlimited) or as companies – but difficulties can arise as the basic commercial structure of these forms of organisation sometimes run counter to the ideals of co-operatives. A slightly modified form is to register the co-operative as a company with liability limited by guarantee. Alternatively, co-operatives can register under the Industrial and Provident Societies Acts 1965-75; this carries with it a number of advantages, including limited liability, but also a number of constraints which members can find irksome. In the past, it has been difficult for members of co-operatives to benefit from ploughing back their profits. However, following changes brought about by the 1986 Finance Act, it is now possible for a high proportion of earnings to be ploughed back, and for workers to share in the resulting growth of assets by the issue of bonus shares free of personal tax.

On the face of it, workers' co-operatives present an attractive proposition. However, promoters must take care that social ideals do not blind them to commercial realities. Anyone interested in forming a workers' co-operative, should firstly contact the Co-operative Development Agency which, among other services, publish a very useful guide:

72 START YOUR OWN BUSINESS

How to Set Up a Co-Operative Business. Its address, and those of other helpful organisations, which can provide help, is shown in Helpline 4.

TOWARDS YOUR BUSINESS PLAN

1 Having fully weighed the pros and cons of the different legal forms of business discussed in this section, which do you think would be most suitable for your proposed business, and why?

2 *If you are opting for a sole proprietorship:*

(a) Are you satisfied that you can cope with the work?

(b) Will you be able to manage as regards finance?

(c) What are the principal problems you anticipate?

3 *If you are opting for a partnership:*

(a) Have you a partner or partners in mind?

(b) Are you satisfied that you can work with them? On what grounds do you make this judgement?

(c) Are you satisfied that the partners will in fact be prepared to 'do their bit?'

Draft out a proposed partnership agreement. Check as soon as possible that your potential partners agree to the provisions.

4 *If you are opting for a company:*
Read the next section before you make a final decision.

5 *If you are thinking of forming a co-operative:*
(a) Have you consulted any of the agencies listed in Helpline 4?

(b) Are you satisfied that you and your colleagues have the basis for a sound *business*?

WHAT LEGAL FORMAT? 73

Can you draw up at this point an outline working constitution to which your colleagues in the co-operative will agree?

THE EIGHTH BIG QUESTION:
Going for the Big Time?

THE NATURE OF A COMPANY

Forming a company is a very different kettle of fish from running a sole proprietorship or a partnership.

It brings you into the big league, and very stringent rules are laid down in the Companies Act 1985 and other legislation as to what must and must not be done. Break the rules, and you could easily find yourself facing big fines, possibly even imprisonment.

Companies are a unique form of business organisation. The main distinction – and there are many others – is that in law the company is quite distinct from the people who formed it and who control it. It is, in fact, a 'legal person' in its own right: this means that it owns its own assets, is normally responsible for its own debts, and can sue and be sued in the courts in its own name. It also means that, unlike partnerships and sole proprietorships, its existence is unaffected by the death of those running it – their shares merely pass to their respective heirs and successors, whilst the company continues.

It is, in fact, quite wrong to talk about shareholders 'owning' a company – they do not. They control it and only own certain rights – such as the right to vote at company meetings and the right to dividends (all of which are subject to the rules of the company) – but they do not own the company as such, or its assets.

Limited liability

The main attraction in forming a company is usually to obtain *limited liability*. This means that once shares have been paid for in full, the shareholder cannot be asked to pay anything more towards the company's debts. However, this advantage may be more illusory than real, for if a newly-formed limited company wants to borrow money, the directors will probably be asked to give a personal guarantee in addition to any security provided by the company, thus making them personally liable. Also, a company in its early days may find it more difficult to obtain credit from its potential suppliers than would a sole trader or partnership.

TAXATION

The possibility – and it is only a possibility – of lower taxation is another attraction. A company is subject to corporation tax, not income tax, though for small companies (i.e. those with taxable profits below £100,000) this is the same rate as the standard rate of income tax (25% in 1988–9). This rises to 35% for companies with profits in excess of £500,000. Unless, therefore, a sole proprietor of a business is paying income tax at the higher rate of 40%, he will not benefit by changing his firm into a company.

Where it is advisable to turn a firm into a company so that the profits are subject to corporation tax and not to the higher rate of income tax, the former proprietors would still be well advised to pay themselves salaries as directors rather than take the total amount as dividends on shares. The salaries would be subject to normal income tax on a PAYE basis, and this enables advantage to be taken of the various personal allowances. The directors should, however, take care that the salaries are not large enough to put them in the higher tax-rate groups.

As with income tax on a partnership's or sole proprietor's profits, corporation tax is not payable until some while after the end of the year in which they were earned. However, if any dividends are paid, what is known as *advance corporation tax* must be paid immediately (this can afterwards be deducted from the corporation tax ultimately due). Also, the income tax due on salaries paid to directors must be deducted immediately under the PAYE regulations, and remitted to the tax office. This, of course, reduces the cash-flow benefits which the delayed payment of corporation tax involves.

Certain special provisions apply to what are known by the Inland Revenue as *close companies*. These are companies under the effective control of five or less people – in other words, the typical 'family firm'.

Some of the disadvantages

There is, though, another side to the coin. A company is much more expensive to set-up than other types of enterprise. Also, the formalities – which have to be followed to the letter, not only on formation but also throughout the life of the company – are much more stringent and demanding. The accounts *must* be audited by an accountant belonging to an approved body, and tax complications arise in carrying forward losses if there is any change in the type of work a company is undertaking. A particular difficulty arises if there are capital gains – for example, if some of the company's land and buildings are sold off at considerable profit – as these may be taxed twice if they are withdrawn from the company. The national insurance contributions of the directors will be considerably greater than if they were partners – but so also will be the benefits.

Company meetings have to be run in accordance with the rules laid down in the Companies Act 1985, and certain decisions require particular types of resolution for which prescribed periods of notice must be given. In addition, a register of members must be maintained, and an annual return made to the Registrar of Companies.

FORMING A COMPANY

Forming a company is a complicated business and advice should first be taken from a chartered company secretary, an accountant or a solicitor, as to whether or not it is advantageous to do so – it may well not be. If it is decided to go ahead and form one, then the legal complications are such that, again, a professional should be asked to do the job.

There are two principal types of companies which can be formed – private ones and public ones. With *public companies*, we are talking about major organisations which must have an issued capital of at least £250,000, and for which a quotation on the stock exchange will probably be sought. This means that, as far as new small businesses are concerned, we are concerned only with *private companies*.

The easiest way to form a private company is to buy a ready-made one 'off the peg'. Company registration agencies have companies already formed which they are prepared to sell as a package deal; these cost from £100 upwards. The company you buy will already have a name; if this is not what you like, it can be changed – for a fee.

The memorandum and articles of association

Companies are regulated by two important documents which must be approved by, and filed with, the Registrar of Companies before formation. These are the memorandum of association and the articles of association.

The *memorandum of association* is a simple document but contains some very important clauses. These include the name of the company, the address of its registered office, the total amount of capital (in the form of shares) that it can issue (this is known as the *authorised capital*), and a statement that the liability of shareholders will be limited. It also contains the *objects clause*. This describes the type of work the company will be undertaking, and it is illegal for the company to operate outside it. There has been much criticism of this clause over recent years and several proposals have been put forward to abandon it – but it is still with us at the moment.

The *articles of association* really amount to the internal working arrangements of the company. They are contained in a much longer document than the memorandum and cover such matters as rights of shareholders, procedure for transfer of shares, how meetings are to be called and run, procedures for voting, powers of directors, the accounting and audit procedures, and the procedure for winding up. Attached to the Companies Act is a model set of articles known as Table A. Instead of writing its own Articles a company can instead adopt Table A, either in whole or in part.

Share capital

Capital is invested in a company by means of buying shares.

There are two main types of shares – preference and ordinary. *Preference shares* carry a 'preferred' dividend; that is, a dividend at a fixed, agreed percentage which must be paid *before* the ordinary shareholders are paid anything. Unless specifically described as non-cumulative, preference shares are regarded as *cumulative*; that is, if the preferred dividend cannot be paid in any one year, it accumulates and must be cleared subsequently before any dividend is paid to ordinary shareholders. It is not normal for preference shares to have any voting rights.

The dividend on *ordinary shares* is decided each year in the light of the profits, and has to be approved at the company's annual general meeting though it is in order for an interim dividend to be paid during the year without this approval.

Dividends *must* be paid out of profits, and only out of profits. It is now illegal for any dividend to be paid to any group of shareholders unless all accumulated losses have been covered by profits.

Loan capital

It is also possible for capital (in the commercial though not strict accounting sense of the word) to be raised by the company borrowing money – either from those who formed it or from outsiders. Loans carry a fixed rate of *interest* which is a legal charge against the company – this means it is deductible from profit before profit is ascertained. It must, in fact, be paid whether the company is running at a profit or a loss. If the loan is evidenced by a formal document which can be transferred to others, it is known as a *debenture*. Debentures and other loans are sometimes secured against a mortgage of the company's assets. Debenture holders do not normally have any voting rights.

Control

The ultimate control of a company lies with the ordinary shareholders. Each ordinary share normally carries one vote. This is important to remember when issuing shares in order to raise capital; the more ordinary shares that are issued to 'outsiders', the greater the risk of losing control. Remember, someone only has to obtain 51% of the vote-carrying shares to have effective control of the company and *all* of its assets.

The day-to-day management is, of course, the responsibility of the directors.

CONCLUSION

There is much to be said both for – and against – forming a company. Whatever else might be said about it, it certainly is not the thing to do by someone who does not know what he is about. If you feel that it may be the thing for you, the advice at this point must be:

> *Think carefully ... and take advice!*

OFFICIAL PUBLICATIONS AVAILABLE FREE FROM:

Stationery Section, Companies Registration Office, Companies House, Maindy, Cardiff CF4 3UZ

	Ref
Incorporation of New Companies	C56
Notes for Guidance of Registered Companies	NG1
Company Names	C57
Limited Partnerships	C428
Notes for Guidance on Business Names and Business Partnerships	NG2
Company and Business Names – Sensitive Words and Expressions	C49

A pack containing all the necessary forms and notes is also available.

TOWARDS YOUR BUSINESS PLAN

1   If you are thinking of forming a company, do you intend to do so

    (a)   from the time you start operations;

    (b)   early in the life of your firm;

    (c)   possibly ultimately, but not immediately?

2   If you are thinking of forming a company in the fairly near future, define precisely what advantages you hope to obtain from it. List the main difficulties or snags which you can foresee.

3   If you are thinking of buying one 'off the peg', check out the cost and the extent to which the package can be made to suit your needs.

4   If you intend to form a company 'from scratch', do you intend to

  (a)   ask a professional to do it for you? If so, whom do you intend to ask? What will be the cost?

  (b)   'do-it-yourself'? In which case, have you sufficient knowledge of company law and practice?

5   Set out a statement of

  (a)   the proposed company name;

  (b)   the amount of authorised capital with which you would register the company;

  (c)   the way the capital would be divided between ordinary and preference shares;

  (d)   how you intend to allocate or sell the shares.

THE NINTH BIG QUESTION:
Finding the Cash

CAPITAL NEEDS

Starting a business almost always involves putting up capital, and associated with that, facing an element of risk. The amount of capital which will be needed, and the degree of risk which will be involved, varies considerably from firm to firm, but there are very few business ideas which do not involve one if not both of these factors.

Finding the capital is usually the biggest problem faced by those intending to start a business. A detailed consideration of the amount of capital likely to be needed, the source from which it is to be obtained, and the cost, must form an essential element of any Business Plan.

If you have been working through this book in the way suggested, you should already have obtained a fairly clear idea of how much capital will be required for the *start-up operation*. It will be the price (by whatever method of purchase you decide upon) of the equipment, stock, premises, initial advertising and marketing, and so on. Unfortunately, it does not stop there, for it may well be some while before your product becomes established and cash starts flowing in – what one might call the *initial survival period*. Once the cash has started coming back, you must then calculate how much capital you will need thereafter for *normal operation*.

When you have calculated those three amounts – but not until then – a serious look can be taken at the second aspect of the problem, namely, how to obtain the capital which will be required.

SOURCES OF FINANCE

Raising capital is never easy: however, it may not be as

difficult as may be feared. There are a number of sources which can be considered.

Own resources

The most obvious source of capital is one's own personal savings. In fact, it is unlikely that other backers will be prepared to take the risk unless the new business owner shows that he has sufficient faith in the project to put his own money into it. The advantage of using one's own money in a venture is that the business remains free of constraints by partners or outside lenders. Nor are the potential profits savaged by burdensome interest charges. However it must not be thought that even one's private money comes 'free' – the cost is the interest which could otherwise be earned by investing it elsewhere, and in the 'opportunity cost' of not being able to do whatever else one would have done with the money. Nevertheless, personal savings are, without doubt, the cheapest form of finance available.

'Own resources' are not limited to savings. An endowment life assurance policy, for example, can be used for raising funds either by surrendering it against a cash settlement, or as security for a loan either from the insurance company or the bank. Caution must be exercised in doing this as it could leave the family without support in the event of the death of the policy holder. A further avenue worth exploring – though one again subject to the same reservation – is a second morgage on the house.

You may, of course, possess some valuable asset or family heirloom which could be sold for cash. But you had better have a word with the family before you do this.

Personal contacts

Capital can sometimes be acquired from or through personal contacts in the form of loans from friends, neighbours or relatives. This has its difficulties as the relative or friend may not like to refuse if approached, yet really not be keen on lending you the money. Many beautiful friendships have ended in this way. Before borrowing from this source, the intending business man has to remember that he may, some day, have to look his friends, neighbours and relatives in the face, and tell them that he has lost their life savings for them. A distinctly unpleasant situation.

Direct participation

It may be possible to persuade a person with capital to become a partner in the business. This would mean that the capital would come interest-free, but that profits would have to be split. This may prove galling if the partner is a 'sleeping' one – i.e. one who does no work in the firm. If a company is formed, it may be possible to sell shares among one's contacts and supporters. If the shares are taken up by one's immediate friends and relatives, there may again be particular embarrassment if the business fails.

Whilst the need to obtain capital may be the paramount consideration, it should never be forgotten that taking on a partner, or the issue of shares, means creating a permanent drain on the profits of the business.

Other loans and grants

Many types of loan and grants are available from specialised institutions; these should always be thoroughly investigated before any decisions are made.

Banks. All the leading commercial banks are very much in the business of lending money and most have special schemes to meet the needs of small business promoters. Competition is intense, and the intending borrower should 'shop around' to find the best terms and conditions.

Once a business is well established and the future looks promising, it may be possible to obtain *venture capital* from a bank – this is where the bank takes a shareholding in the business. It is not usually available if conventional loans can be obtained, and is normally limited to established companies of reasonable size.

Local authorities. Most local authorities have special schemes to encourage the development of new small businesses

If borrowing money, ask these questions

- Will the interest rate be fixed or variable?
- Will the interest be based upon the sum originally borrowed or on the balance outstanding from day-to-day?
- What 'collateral' (i.e. security) security will be required.
- What 'service' costs (e.g. valuation fees, mortgage stamp duties) will be payable?
- Is the loan for a definite fixed period or can it be called in at short notice?
- What are the amounts and dates of the repayments?
- Will there be a *capital repayment holiday* of any type to enable the business to get established before having to find the repayments?

within their areas. The nature of the help varies considerably, and there may be restrictions on the type of businesses which qualify. Contact should be made with the local authority concerned as early as possible to see what the possibilities are.

Rural Development Commission Business Service (formerly CoSIRA – Council for Small Industries in Rural Areas). This is a government agency which offers help to small enterprises in rural areas and towns of less than 10,000 inhabitants. In conjunction with Lloyds Bank, loans of up to £1 million may be made for periods of up to thirty years with repayment schemes tailored to meet the needs and problems of the firm concerned – including, in some instances, a capital repayment holiday of up to two years. A Business Loan Repayment Insurance Scheme is also operated to safeguard borrowers and their families in the event of injury or death. Specialised advice is also available covering business management, skills training, technical help, production management, marketing and publicity.

Small Firms Loan Guarantee Scheme. Certain types of businesses which are unable to raise finance through normal sources because of lack of security may be eligible for a guarantee under this scheme which will enable them to obtain a loan from one of the participating banks. The scheme was introduced in 1981 and is operated by the Department of Industry. The guarantee covers 70% of approved loans for amounts up to £75,000 repayable over two to seven years. Guarantees are not normally available to cover overdrafts or for loans below £5,000. The assets of the business must be pledged as security for the loan, personal guarantees not being acceptable. The interest charged is slightly higher than the bank's base rate and an arrangement fee is payable; there may also be additional security fees relating to the charges over the assets together with a premium (currently $2\frac{1}{2}$%) on the outstanding amount of the guaranteed portion of the loan. All applications have to be accompanied by a detailed business plan, together with cash flow and profits forecasts for two years.

Industrial Common Ownership Finance Ltd Loan Scheme. The ICOF operates a revolving loan scheme specifically for enterprises set up on a co-operative basis. The scheme covers loans of £1,000 to £35,000, though borrowers are expected to provide some of the funds required themselves.

Enterprise Allowance Scheme. This scheme is designed to help unemployed people who wish to start up their own business but who are concerned that by so doing they will lose their entitlement to unemployment or supplementary benefit. Applicants must be aged over 18 and under 65, have been unemployed for at least 13 weeks and be receiving unemployment or supplementary benefit. They themselves must put at least £1,000 into the business, which must be new, independent and likely to employ not more than 20 people during the first three months. The scheme consists of an allowance, not a loan, of £40 a week (taxable) for a maximum of 52 weeks.

Enterprise Zones. Special help is given to enterprises in these areas by way of allowances on commercial and industrial buildings in relation to corporation tax and income tax. Relief, and sometimes exemption, is sometimes allowed from general rates. Government policy in relation to these zones is in process of change, and the current position as it is likely to affect small firms should be checked out with the Small Firms Service.

The Department of Employment is able to help new businesses in a number of different ways, one of which is by financial contributions towards training costs. This service was, until recently, administered through the Training Commission. A pack of information, including up-to-date pamphlets on all the schemes, is available to anyone considering setting up their own business from the Department's Public Enquiry Point (see p. 87).

Other forms of financial help available include the following:

Factoring. The idea behind factoring is that the trade debts due to a firm are sold to a factoring agency which becomes responsible for collecting the amount due. The normal arrangement is that all debts arising from credit sales are handed over to the factor who, if required, will immediately pay the firm concerned up to 80% of the sums concerned. The balance will be paid after collection. The commission varies with the risk involved – usually between 0.5% and 2.5% – and normal lending rates are charged on any sums paid to the seller before collection. Factoring agencies normally expect to deal with the whole of a firm's credit sales on a regular basis – not just those likely to prove doubtful – and only deal with firms with annual turnovers of £200,000 or more. Your bank manager can usually put you in touch with a reliable agency. Check carefully what it will cost you before you commit yourself.

Hire purchase/leasing. The burden of the cost of major assets can be eased by financing the purchase through one of the many hire-purchase or lease-hire facilities readily available through suppliers, or by simple credit purchase. These schemes were discussed on pp.52-53.

Credit cards. Small firms should not ignore the value to be obtained by the *prudent* use of credit and charge cards. By careful use of these, it is possible to gain short-term interest-free credit provided the debt is settled promptly within the period laid down. The credit is not interest-free if the card is used to obtain a cash advance, and if the debt is allowed to remain unpaid for longer than the stipulated period. Indeed, used in such a way, a credit card can be an extremely expensive way of borrowing money.

Some useful addresses

Rural Development Commission Business Service (formerly CoSIRA)
141 Castle Street, Salisbury, Wilts SP1 3TP
(0722 336255)
For *local office*, consult telephone directory or local branch of Lloyds Bank)

Department of Trade and Industry
Kingsgate House, 66-74 Victoria Street, London SW1E 6SG (01 215 4121)

Loans Guarantee Unit
Room 221, Steel House, Tothill Street, London SW1H 9NF (01 273 3000)

ICIF Ltd
4 St Giles Street, Northampton NN1 1AA (0604 37563)

Department of Employment/Manpower Services Commission
Public Enquiry Point, Room N1110, Moorfoot, Sheffield S1 4PQ (0742 704318) (*NOTE: The country is covered by regional offices; the addresses and phone numbers of these can be found in the local telephone directory. It is possible that they will be listed under the old name, i.e. the Manpower Services Commission.*)

CONSUMER CREDIT ACT 1976

The Consumer Credit Act is a long and very involved statute and covers the provision of finance to individuals and unincorporated bodies such as partnerships. It does not apply to credit given to companies. Its purpose is to protect borrowers from unscrupulous lenders; any loan covered by the act has to be fully documented, with copies being provided to the borrower who is entitled to a 'consideration period' i.e. time in which to reconsider and cancel the arrangement. The act also requires a clear and fair statement of all costs to be paid by the borrower (known as the *total charge for credit*) and must be expressed in the form of an *annual percentage rate of charge (the APR)*. The act sets out very precise rules for the calculation of this figure which is aimed at giving a *true* indication of what the real cost of borrowing will be – in the past, this has often been covered up by describing and calculating interest rates on the sums originally borrowed not the actual rate paid on the amount owed from day to day. Also, many of the additional 'service' and other charges have not been made clear; all of these must now be clearly stated, and have to be taken into account in calculating the APR.

The act does *not*, however, apply to overdraft arrangements from banks. This makes it extremely important, should you be considering overdraft finance, to find out from the bank exactly what the cost will be; indeed, confirmation of this in writing should be asked for.

In conclusion, REMEMBER:

LOAN CAPITAL NEVER COMES CHEAP

ANTICIPATED RETURNS MUST BE CHECKED CAREFULLY AGAINST THE COST

CONSIDER CAREFULLY BEFORE YOU COMMIT YOURSELF

Note: Conditions and regulations relating to loans change periodically. Check the information in this book with the appropriate body before making any plans or decisions.

TOWARDS YOUR BUSINESS PLAN

You should now be in a position to draw up a detailed capital budget showing

    (a)   HOW MUCH capital you will need and for what purpose; and

    (b)   WHEN you will need it.

Add a clear statement outlining exactly how you propose obtaining the amounts needed.

Draw this budget up carefully as it will be subjected to very close scrutiny by any organisation from which you propose to borrow money.

THE TENTH BIG QUESTION:

Accounting for the Cash

Before commencing business, it is vital that your firm has an adequate system of accounting. This is necessary in order to provide:

(a) a day-by-day record of all financial activities; and

(b) the end-of-year summaries – usually called the 'final accounts'.

If you are thinking of starting a business, there is one golden rule in accounting which you must remember. It is simply this:

Always keep the firm's financial affairs distinct from your own

This means that the firm (or firm-to-be) must have a bank account *of its own*, and that the firm's cash-in-hand should never *ever* get muddled with your own personal cash-in-pocket.

Confuse the firm's affairs with your own, and you are on the highroad to disaster.

From that point on, there are two things you can do. One is to set up and operate your own system. To do this, you – or the person you employ to do the job for you – will obviously have to know something about accounting. The alternative is to invest in one of the 'off-the-shelf' prepackaged accounting systems which are on the market.

'OFF THE SHELF' PACKAGES

If you do not know much about accounting, there is much to be said for purchasing one of the simpler ready-made accounting systems which are on the market. These systems fall into three main groups.

The first group are the *wholly 'manual' systems* which consist of a set of printed books and forms. The business owner fills in the detailed information where instructed and, step by step, he is led through the principal accounting procedures up to, and sometimes including, the preparation of the final accounts.

The second group consists of what are sometimes called *'three in one' systems*. These make use of specially designed boards on which pre-printed stationery is clipped. NCR (no carbon required) paper is used; this means that carbon-like copies are obtained although no carbon paper is used. Again, by following the instructions, the basic processes are completed. The board aligns the carbon copies so that several operations can be completed simultaneously – hence the idea of 'three operations by one entry' (misleading because quite often more than three operations are completed). These systems are, naturally, slightly more expensive than purely manual systems.

The third group consist of the wide range of *computer accounting packages* which are now on the market, many designed especially for the small firm. They consist of an accounting framework set up by experts into which the business owner feeds the data relating to his own firm. Not only will the relevant accounts and backing documentation (such as invoices, delivery notes and statements) be produced but various other tasks – such as stock control and checks on the age of debts – can be done. Computerised systems are very much quicker and more efficient than other systems, but their cost – both of the machine itself and of the software to go with it – is very much greater.

One of the problems in setting up a new firm is that its needs and requirements are often not fully known at the start, and may ultimately prove to be different from those initially anticipated. This means that it may be unwise to invest considerable sums in highly sophisticated systems until it is known that there is a need for them. Also, of course, as firms grow, so also do needs. A business which only needs a manual system today, may well need a three-in-one system tomorrow, and a computerised system in the not too distant future. No business wants to have more changes in its accounting and administrative system than necessary,

92 START YOUR OWN BUSINESS

Dr		(DEBIT) (RECEIPTS)		Cash a/c				(PAYMENTS)	Cr (CREDIT)	
Jan	1	Balance	b/d	1000	–	Jan	6	Insurance	150	–
"	2	Hairdressing receipts		120	56	"	8	Advertising	75	–
"	3	Sales of shampoos etc		52	10	"	9	Insurance	10	–
"	5	Hairdressing receipts		200	09					
"	8	" "		130	10					
"	9	Sales of shampoos etc		34	20					

Figure 4 A simple form of cash account (a hairdresser's)

Dr				Cash a/c					Cr	
Jan	1	Balance	b/d	1000	–	Jan	6	Insurance	150	–
"	2	Hairdressing receipts		120	56	"	8	Advertising	75	–
"	3	Sales of shampoos etc		52	10	"	9	Insurance	10	–
"	5	Hairdressing receipts		200	09	"	9	Balance	c/d	1302	05
"	8	" "		130	10					
"	9	Sales of shampoos etc		34	20					
				1537	05				1537	05
Jan	10	Balance	b/d	1302	05					

Figure 5 The hairdresser's cash account now balanced, with the balance in hand at the close of business on 9 January carried down to the opening of business on 10 January

but the system must keep in step with needs. One company which has come to terms with this is Kalamazoo which has developed a very cheap and easy-to-follow manual system (the 'Book-keeper' system) which, as a firm grows, can easily be converted into a three-in-one system, and this in turn into a complete computerised system. Details can be obtained from Kalamazoo, Northfield, Birmingham B31 2RW (021 411 2345).

Before committing yourself to a purchase of *any* mechanised or computerised system, re-read pp. 49–51 again.

BASIC CASH ACCOUNTING

Whether you buy an 'off-the-shelf' package, or you devise your own system, any business owner should understand the basic mechanics of book-keeping. At the heart of any accounting system are the cash and bank records. They are obviously important, in themselves, for any firm which does not maintain a very close control on its cash-flow will very

			Dr		Cr		Balance	
Jan	1	Balance					1000	—
	2	Hairdressing receipts	120	56			1120	56
	3	Sale of shampoos etc	52	10			1172	66
	5	Hairdressing receipts	200	09			1372	75
	6	Insurance			150	—	1222	75
	8	Hairdressing receipts	130	10			1312	85
	8	Advertising			75	—	1277	85
	9	Sale of shampoos	34	20			1312	05
	10	Insurance			10	—	1302	05

Figure 6 Running balance cash account

soon be in trouble. They can also provide much of the additional information which is needed if proper accounts are to be maintained. There are several different forms which cash and bank records can take.

Simple cash accounts

The one thing no firm can get by without is a proper record of cash receipts and payments. Any busines owner should know enough about accounting to keep his cash records up-to-date, and indeed he will be courting disaster if he does not. Also, given satisfactory cash records plus certain supplementary information, then an accountant will have no trouble in preparing the end-of-year final accounts.

Although it is possible to keep a record of cash receipts and payments in a simple notebook with one cash column, it is cumbersome and likely to lead to error because receipts and payments can easily get muddled. It is therefore better to record the transactions in conventional ledger account form. This consists of a page divided down the middle, with a cash column on each half. There are also columns for the date of the transaction, and a 'details' column which gives a brief explanation of the transaction concerned. There is also, usually, a small 'folio' column which can be used for cross-referencing. All of the simple manual systems rely on this form of account.

The left-hand side of the page the *debit* (Dr) side is used to record receipts of cash, and the right hand side the *credit* (Cr) side is used for payments. An example is shown in Figure 4. The 'details' column of the debit side indicates from where the cash receipts have come, whilst the corresponding column on the debit side shows on what the cash has been spent.

Provided, of course, that every item is entered on the correct side, there is little chance of confusion between receipts and payments. Unfortunately this form of account does not show immediately what the balance is. This can only be found by 'balancing'. This entails:

(a) finding the difference between the two sides;

(b) entering this figure on the 'lighter' of the two sides;

(c) adding the two columns to prove that the balance entered is, indeed, the correct figure (*it is important that the two totals should appear on the same level, even if it means leaving a space on one side or the other*);

(d) entering the balance figure again, this time below the totals on the 'heavier' of the two sides.

The 'balanced' account is shown in Figure 5. Notice the abbreviations c/d (meaning '(to be) carried down') and b/d (meaning '(it has been) brought down'). If carrying a balance over the page, it is conventional to use the abbreviations c/f (carried forward) and b/f (brought forward) respectively.

Running-balance accounts

An alternative form of account is the 'running balance' one. This has three columns – the first for debit entries, the second for credit entries, and the third for the balance which is entered up after each transaction. This format is shown in Figure 6.

This form has the obvious advantage that the balance is shown after every entry. It is, however, time-consuming and mistakes can easily occur – and once made, they are carried forward in balance after balance. This means that running balance accounts are really only practical if machines are available to undertake the job. Bank statements (copies of the account of a person or firm in the books of the bank) are presented in this way. (The entries which appear in the *debit* column of the firm's own record of cash-at-bank will appear in the *credit* column of the bank statement; also, the items which appear in the *credit* column of the firm's books, will appear in the *debit* column of the bank statement. This is because the bank is showing 'their' side of the transaction, not that of the firm. When money is paid into the bank, the bank becomes the firm's *debtor* and this is what is shown in the firm's books. The customer, however, becomes the bank's *creditor*, and this is what the bank's records show.)

Analysed cash records

It will be essential, for the final accounts, to know how much is paid out on *each* major item of expense. It may also be necessary to analyse receipts, though with many small firms this is likely to be from one main source only – newly trading receipts. Although this information is, in fact, given in the 'details' column of the ledger, it is tedious to have to go back over – perhaps – hundreds of entries and split them up according to the main heads of expenditure. A quick and efficient way for a small firm to obtain the information quickly and efficiently is to have a cash account with analysis columns. This involves having one main, or 'totals' column, plus additional columns across the page headed for each major item of expense. The item is then entered both in the 'totals' column and again in the appropriate 'analysis' column. The advantages of this system is that:

(a) both 'total and 'analysed' totals are shown;

(b) each page can be 'cross-cast' – that is added horizontally to check that the individual totals add up to the 'totals' column – thus proving the accuracy of the work.

Figure 7 shows an example of an analysed cash book. The needs of firms as regards the number of columns 'on each side' will of course vary, but any good stationer will have in stock accounting paper (both in looseleaf and in bound book form) with a wide variety of rulings.

Accounting for cash at the bank

The record of cash at the bank is maintained in exactly the same way as cash-in-hand, and the same options concerning rulings are available. The record may be kept separately from the cash account, or the two can be combined into one book. This is known as the two-column cash book which has two separate columns on each of the two sides of the account – one for cash and one for bank items. The respective columns are balanced independently, and each balance carried down to the next period. This cash book may consist simply of the unanalysed cash and bank columns (Figure 8) or it, too, can have additional analysis columns on either or both sides.

A further variant is the three-column cash book, the

ACCOUNTING FOR THE CASH

			TOTAL	HAIR DRESSING	SALES	OTHER				TOTAL	WAGES	INSUR-ANCE	ADVERT-ISING	TELE-PHONE	RENT	OTHER
Jan	1	Balance	1000			1000 -	Jan	6	Insurance	150 -	150 -					
	2	Receipts	120 56	120 56				8	Advertising	75 -			75 -			
	3	Sales	52 10		52 10			9	Insurance	10 -		10 -				
	5	Receipts	200 09	200 09				9	Balance c/d	1302 05						1302 05
	8	Sales	130 10	130 10												
	9	Sales	34 20		34 20											
	9	Sales	86 30		86 30					1537 05		160 -	75 -			1302 05
			1537 05	450 75	86 30	1000 -										
Jan	10	Balance b/d	1302 05													

Figure 7 Analysed cash book

Note: Normally the balances of the analysis columns would be carried forward until the end of the accounting year.

			CASH	BANK				CASH	BANK
Mar	1	Balances	b/d	250 -	7261 48	Mar	3	Star Insurance Co.		500 -
	4	Cash sales	360 -			7	Wetherfield Advertiser (advertising)		60 -
	6	Cash sales	840 -			9	Electricity Board		100 -
	8	T. Jones (debtor)		380 20		11	Cash paid into bank	1820 -	
	10	Cash sales	620 -			11	Balances	c/d	250 -	8801 68
	11	Cash paid into bank		1820 -				2070 -	9461 68
			2070 -	9461 68					
	11	Balances	b/d	250 -	8801 68					

Figure 8 Two-column cash book

third column being used to record the discount associated with the respective receipts and payments.

OTHER ESSENTIAL RECORDS

There are other important records which will be absolutely necessary for the efficient day-to-day running of the firm and for the drawing up of the final accounts at the end of the year. If a full double-entry accounting system is being maintained, the information will be forthcoming automatically. In the absence of such a system, it is essential that records be kept of:

Credit sales

If goods are being sold in credit, then records will have to be kept of the amount sold to each individual customer. These individual records will also have to record all goods returned by the customer, discounts allowed to him, and any payments received from him. Only by doing this can a proper day-by-day control of debtors be maintained of the debts owed to the firm.

It will also prove worthwhile to keep a record of the cumulative amount sold on credit to all customers during the year. Both this figure, and the total value of debts as at the end of the year, will be needed for the final accounts.

Those with accounting knowledge will recognise the basics here of a sales ledger.

A separate record should be maintained of any debts which it is decided to write off as 'bad'.

Credit purchases

Similarly, a record must be maintained of all credit purchases, together with the detail of the amount purchased from each individual supplier. Against these individual amounts will have to be set any goods returned, any payments to him and any discount received from him. This will provide the records of the debts which need paying day-by-day, as well as the total figure for credit purchases at the end of the year.

In this file, of course, we have the elements of the purchases ledger.

Stock

The importance of keeping stock records as an on-going operation has already been emphasised (see p. 33). Those records, however, were primarily concerned with keeping track of *quantities* in hand, not their *money values*.

The day-to-day money side of things is recorded through the records of sales and purchases mentioned above, but these two figures cannot be used to calculate the value of stock on hand at the end of the year. This is because purchases are recorded at cost price, whilst sales are recorded at selling price, and the two just cannot be mixed.

This means that, unless each sale has been recorded at its cost price *as well as* its selling price (usually so time-consuming as to be impracticable), there will have to be a physical stock-take at the end of the year to ascertain exactly what is still in hand. This stock is then valued at its original cost (unless the replacement cost is less). For this purpose, it is usually assumed that stock has been used on a *FIFO* (first in, first out) basis i.e. that the stock left over is that which has been bought most recently.

Expenses owed and paid in advance

If a correct figure is to be obtained for the various expenses incurred during the year, the amount actually paid (picked up from the analysed cash book) may have to be modified. Any amount owing in respect of the item at the end of the year (known as an *accrual*) will have to be added (otherwise you would be making a bigger profit because you were not paying your bills), and any amount paid in advance for the following year (known as a *prepayment*) will have to be deducted. These adjustments will, of course, be carried forward and will affect the figures for the following year.

In some cases – e.g. rents, rates, insurances and wages – it will be possible to calculate the amounts exactly. In the case of others – e.g. electricity charges – it will be necessary to make a rough calculation.

Other assets and liabilities

If a true summary of your financial position is to be prepared at the end of the financial year, a record will have to be kept of the current value (i.e. original cost less depreciation) of each individual asset. There will also have to be a note of liabilities other than trade creditors – for example, long-term liabilities such as loans.

Unusual items

Finally, a list should be kept, with details, of any 'unusual' items as they occur – such as loss of stock by theft or by fire.

WHAT DOES IT ALL ADD UP TO?

At the end of the firm's financial year, two summaries will have to be prepared. The first is a trading and profit and loss account for the year. This will show the gross profit – this is the difference between the sales income, and the cost of the goods which have been sold. It will also show the net profit, which is the gross profit less all the other expenses. The sales income will be that which has been *earned* within the period, not that which has actually been received. The expenses, similarly, will be those which have been *incurred*, whether or not they have been paid.

The second is a statement of the firm's financial position on the last day of the financial year. This will summarise the assets owned at that date, and the debts owed to others. The difference will be the net worth of the firm as at that date – in accounting terms, the firm's capital.

To draw up these summaries correctly requires a good knowledge of accounting. Unless you have that knowledge, you would be well advised to ask an accountant to do the job for you. He will, at the same time, ensure that the proper returns are made to the Inland Revenue and that you claim all the allowances to which you are entitled. His job will, however, be made immeasurably simpler if reliable basic records similar to those outlined above are available.

TOWARDS YOUR BUSINESS PLAN

1 Attempt an analysis of your accounting problem:

    (a)   what cash will you be receiving?

    (b)   how are you going to
          (i) handle it from a security point of view
          (ii) record it from an accounting point of view?

    (c)   what 'system' do you plan for payments?

2 Consider how much of the accounting can you do for yourself. Bear in mind the need for both (i) the necessary knowlege and (ii) the time it will take. What plans do you suggest for coping with that which you cannot do for yourself?

3 If you intend to undertake the accounting yourself, do you have a sufficient knowledge of tax as regards:

    (a)   PAYE procedures (schedule E income tax)

    (b)   tax of the firm's profits (schedule D income tax)

    (c)   corporation tax if you intend to form a company?

What about national insurance?

If not, what can you do about it?

4 Summarise your plans for recording credit sales and purchases.

5 Outline how you plan to monitor the debts owed to you. What will be your standard procedure for 'bad debts'?

THE TENTH BIG QUESTION ... continued:
Some Particular Accounting Problems

Coping with the routine book-keeping is not the only accounting problem a business manager has to deal with. In addition, there are a number of procedures which, although peripheral to the keeping of the accounts as such, are equally important.

CHECKING THE BANK STATEMENT

It will be necessary, from time to time, to check the statement received from the bank with the firm's own record of bank balances. As mentioned above, the bank statement will be in 'running balance' form, and the entries will be in the 'opposite columns to those in the firm's own record.

There will almost certainly appear to be differences between the bank record kept by the firm, and the bank statement. This will be for a number of reasons. Cheques drawn and entered in the firm's records may not have been presented to the bank for payment by the date of the bank statement. The firm may have forgotten to enter up standing order payments, or may not have recorded direct debits. In addition, the bank may well have deducted bank charges from the final balance, and the first the firm will know of this is when the statement is received. Finally, the firm – or indeed the bank – may well have made mistakes in the account.

The check is therefore necessary:

(a) to ascertain the true up-to-date balance, and

(b) to confirm that, when all matters are taken into account, the two documents are really saying the same thing.

SOME PARTICULAR ACCOUNTING PROBLEMS 103

On receipt of a bank statement, three things must be done. The first is to *check the debit of the bank account in the firm's books*, with the credit column of the bank statement, noting any item which does not appear in both documents. The same must also be done with the credit column of the firm's record, and the debit of the bank statement.

The second is that the *firm should up-date its own records* with all the items which appear only on the bank statement.

The third step is to *up-date the figure given on the bank statement* by adjusting it for the items which appear in the firm's books, but not on the statement. The up-dated bank statement figure should, of course, match the up-dated figure in the firm's own books. (This task can be attempted by drawing up what is known as a *bank reconciliation statement*. The procedure just mentioned is, however, simpler and quite sufficient for the efficient operation of a small firm.)

WAGE PROCEDURES

If a small business intends to employ staff, it will be faced with the payment of wages. There are three distinct aspects to the problem:

(a) maintaining the routine 'back-up' records from which the wages can be prepared;

(b) preparing the actual wage sheets;

(c) making the actual wage payments to the staff concerned.

The *back-up records* will vary according to the type and size of the firm, and the basis on which staff are paid. There should, at the very least, be a file of personnel which will record, for each individual the relevant personal details such as the scale and current rate of pay, the tax code number and any other relevant details, such as agreements, signed by the worker concerned, to any deductions from wages other than statutory (tax and national insurance) ones. The personnel file should also record a note concerning paid holiday entitlements and agreed overtime rates.

Where workers are paid on a 'time' basis and their hours are likely to vary, there will have to be some form of

104 START YOUR OWN BUSINESS

'time card' for each worker concerned which will record the hours worked each day.

The *wage sheet*, or pay roll, is the document on which the wages payable to each employee are calculated. It shows the gross wage, the various deductions, and the net wage payable. There is an additional column for the employer's contribution to each employee's national insurance. As

WEEK/MONTH ENDING:	NAME	HOURS WORKED	RATE PER HOUR	GROSS WAGE	NATIONAL INSURANCE (EMPLOYEE'S CONTRIBUTION)	INCOME TAX	NET WAGE	NATIONAL INSURANCE (EMPLOYER'S CONTRIBUTION)

Figure 9 Simple form of wage sheet

regards any other deductions – such as trade union subscriptions or private pension fund contributions, remember that, as a general rule, it is illegal to make deductions from an employee's wage (other than for tax and national insurance), without that employee's written consent. A simple form of wage sheet is shown in Figure 9.

The tax and insurance calculations involve a relatively complex procedure. Unless you are familiar with it already, you would probably be best advised to employ someone who knows what they are doing, possibly on a part-time basis, to prepare the wage sheets for you.

The national insurance position has been complicated by the complex legislation which came into force in July 1988. This permits an employee – under certain conditions – to 'contract out' of the state pension scheme and contribute instead to an approved personal pension scheme. It also permits businesses to run their own 'in company schemes' which have certain tax advantages. However, a new small firm is not likely to be in a position to run its own scheme. The best procedure in the initial stages is probably to inform employees that the firm will make deductions under SERPS (state earnings related pension scheme) unless the employee himself or herself wishes to contract out in favour of a personal scheme. Should the employees wish to do that, then the firm should arrange for the employee to be advised by a responsible and independent broker – preferably a member of the British Insurance and Investment Brokers Association (address on page 66) – who is authorised to give advice under the Financial Services Act.

Employers are, of course, under a strict legal obligation to ensure that tax and insurance deductions, including the employer's own contribution, are paid over to the State.

As regard actual *wage payment*, it is safer and more satisfactory for all concerned if arrangements can be made for the amounts due to be paid by cheque, or alternatively credited directly to workers' bank accounts. Bank managers will, of course, discuss arrangements for this. If, however, wages do have to be paid in cash, then ensure that as many security measures are taken as possible – see Display p.106. A pay statement, showing the gross amount and all deductions, must be given to each employee.

Paying wages in cash: Some Simple Safeguards

- Collect from the bank the EXACT amount of the wages to be paid out.
- Ensure that you collect sufficient 'small change' – if possible, calculate the exact amount of each denomination of coin that you will need.
- Vary the time and your route to and from the bank to collect the money. Ensure two people go together (not always the same two) and that a car is used if possible. Better still, use the services of a security firm if you can afford it.
- Rotate the staff responsible for making up the wage packets.
- Cash collected from bank should, of course, be exactly the amount required for the pay packets – any amount left over, or any shortage, indicates a mistake has been made. Ensure sufficient time is left before 'pay-out' time to check for errors. Do not seal envelopes until satisfied all correct.
- Require two staff (at least, and not always the same two) to be present at pay-out who should sign the wage sheets.
- Employees should sign for wages collected. An employee should not normally be allowed to collect the wages of another employee. If this is allowed, it should only be done against a signed authorisation.
- Wages not collected should be returned to the safe. There should be a periodic check on reasons for non-collection.

NB: The system and the safeguards employed will vary considerably with the size of the firm, and the number of employees and wages staff involved.

VALUE ADDED TAX (VAT)

VAT is a tax which, put simply, most business firms

are required to add to their own price and to remit to the Customs and Excise Department. VAT tax, and anyone seriously intending to start a business should contact their local VAT office (look under Customs and Excise in the phone book) at as early a stage as possible – certainly before business is commenced.

The general principle of VAT is that every firm in the distribution chain – from the manufacturer down to the retailer – charges a tax on the 'value he has added' to the goods. The amount of the tax is based on the difference between the price at which the firm bought the goods or services, and the price at which it sells them. This is achieved, in practice, by the firm concerned paying the agreed rate of VAT tax on the selling price of the goods (known at the *output* tax), but reclaiming the tax paid when the goods were bought (the *input* tax).

Not all firms are subject to the tax; some rank as *'exempt' firms*. This means that they do not *have* to register, unless their taxable turnover (i.e. total sales subject to VAT) is in excess of a particular figure (during 1988/89 £22,100). If a firm does not register, it does not have to add the tax to its goods, but neither can it claim back the input tax.

Not all goods and services are subject to the tax. Although most are 'standard rated' (15% in 1988-9), some are 'zero-rated' and some are 'exempt'. In the case of both zero-rated and exempt goods, no tax is chargeable, but differences arise over the amount of input tax which can be reclaimed. Some very fine distinctions are drawn as to which goods are standard rated, which are zero-rated and which are exempt. Again, it must be emphasised, advice should be sought as early as possible from the local VAT office.

VAT is charged on the invoice price of goods net after both trade and cash discount have been deducted. Since VAT has to be stated on the invoice, it has to be assumed that the cash discount will in due time be allowed. Even if it is not, and the customer pays the full amount, the VAT is not altered. The VAT returns are, in fact, made up from the invoices and paid accordingly irrespective of how long it takes to get the money from the customer – in fact, it must still be paid even if the debt is ultimately written off as 'bad' and never, in fact, paid.

Business owners are required by law to maintain 'adequate and proper' records to support their VAT returns and VAT officers have the power to call and inspect them. Heavy penalties exist if the regulations are infringed.

Let it be emphasised again; *take advice early*.

HELPLINE 5

The following pamphlets will be found helpful:

Obtainable from your local tax office:

Employer's Guide to Pay As You Earn (P7 [1987]) and *Supplement* (P7S [1988])

Thinking of Working for Yourself? (IR 57)

Thinking of Taking Someone On? PAYE for Employers (IR 53)

Starting in Business (IR 28)

Obtainable from your local office of the Department of Health and Social Security

National Insurance Guide for the Self-employed (NI 41)

National Insurance for Employees (NI 40)

National Insurance Contribution Rates, Statutory Sick Pay and Statutory Maternity Pay Rates (NI 208)

Obtainable from the local VAT office (H.M. Customs and Excise)

The VAT Guide (700)

The Ins and Outs of VAT (700/15A/87)

Should I be Registered for VAT? (700/1/87)

Filling In Your VAT Form (700/12/87)

Visits by VAT Officers (700/26/86)

VAT Publications (700/13/88)

In addition, each Department has a wide range of pamphlets on specialised aspects and problems.

SOME PARTICULAR ACCOUNTING PROBLEMS

INSURANCES

In addition to normal commercial risks, business organisations constantly face other hazards – such as those arising from fire, flood, theft, accident, and negligence. The nature of the firm and its work will determine the range of insurances which it will be advisable to carry, and the extent of the cover on each one. Under-insurance as well as lack of insurance can endanger the future of a firm. The more obvious risks against which cover should be considered are shown below. The importance of obtaining the advice of an independent broker cannot be overemphasised (see p.66 for the address of the BIIBA).

Insurance – what cover will you need?

(a) *Employers' liability*, covering claims by employees following injury or disease resulting from work.

(b) *Motor insurance*. Vehicles must be insured at least against third party claims. If private vehicles are used within the firm, the normal insurance will have to be extended.

(c) *Engineering equipment insurance* covering plant and machinery against risks such as collapse, explosion and breakdown. This is particularly important where pressure equipment is in use.

(d) *Fire insurance*, covering buildings, contents, stock and work-in-progress. Extra cover can be taken for damage from lightning, explosions, aircraft, earthquake, storm, flood, water damage, impact, riot, civil commotion and malicious damage.

(e) *Insurance against theft*, where there has been forcible entry, actual or threatened violence. Theft by dishonesty without some element of force is not usually covered. Additional policies can be taken to cover this.

(f) *Insurance against money loss*. Insurers will probably insist on sensible precautions being taken to reduce the risk of this loss.

(g) *Insurance of goods in transit.* A wide range of policies exist to cover the various risks involved and the different types of cover required.

(h) *Insurance against consequential loss,* such as loss of profits as a result of fire or flood. The policy can cover wages of laid-off employees and temporary additional working costs.

(i) *Credit insurance* provides against non-payment by creditors.

(j) *Public liability* provides covers against claims by the general public for loss arising as a result of the firm's activities.

(k) *Professional indemnity* covers against negligence claims arising from faulty professional advice.

(l) *Product liability* covers claims arising from faulty goods.

(m) *Legal expenses insurance* covers cost of legal advice and representation.

A wide range of specialised policies also exist, such as glass breakage, frozen foods and other stock deterioration, computers and computer records, and business machines and equipment. Cover can also be obtained in respect of specialised types of work and operations.

AUDIT

Companies must, by law, have their annual accounts audited by a properly qualified accountant. There is no such requirement for sole proprietorships or partnerships but, if they have been properly audited, they are more likely to be accepted without query by the Inland Revenue.

CASH BUDGETS

All the accounting procedures we have looked at so far have been concerned with recording what has happened *in the past* – what in the trade is called *historical accounting*. The importance of doing this must not be underrated – but just as important from a management point of view (perhaps even

SOME PARTICULAR ACCOUNTING PROBLEMS 111

more important) is to forecast what is likely to happen in the foreseeable future. Whenever an estimate is made of the future, it is known as a *budget*. A *production budget* estimates the week-by-week (or month-by-month) levels of production

Month	January		February		March	
	Budget £	Actual £	Budget £	Actual £	Budget £	Actual £
Opening balance	3,800	3,800	3,350	1,200	1,250	
Receipts						
Cash	12,000	10,000	13,000		14,000	
Debtors	15,000	13,000	14,000		13,000	
Other						
TOTAL RECEIPTS	30,800	26,800	30,350		28,250	
Payments						
Cash purchases	1,500	2,200	4,500		2,000	
Creditors	21,000	19,000	25,000		24,000	
Net wages	800	800	800		800	
PAYE	150	150	150		150	
Tax (Schedule D)	3,000	3,000	−		−	
Electricity	150	200	200		200	
Office expenses	100	150	250		200	
Rent & rates	−	−	−		2,000	
Advertising	250	100	200		100	
Other						
New Cash Till			1,000			
TOTAL PAYMENTS	27,450	25,600	29,100		29,450	
CLOSING BALANCE	3,350	1,200	1,250		(1,200)	

Figure 10 Cash budget

This figure illustrates a simple cash budget of a trader prepared in December for the first three months of the following year. Assume that the time is the end of January, and that the trader has been able to enter up the actual amounts for that month.

Has the trader a foreseeable problem?
What is it?
What action should he take – and when?

over the coming months; the *marketing budget* consists of a similar estimate for sales. From these, plans can be made for the purchasing of raw materials and for the storage of stock. These budgets will also indicate the likely needs for cash, and the likely receipts.

This brings us to the most crucial of all the budgets, namely the *cash budget*. The cash budget is a projection of the expected flow of cash coming in, and the anticipated expenditure, for the period ahead.

A cash flow budget lists:

(a) all the anticipated cash income, from all sources, month by month (or even week by week depending upon the detail of information available and needed);

(b) all anticipated expenditure;

(c) the balance of cash available at the end of each of the sub-periods.

An example of a cash budget is shown in Figure 10. Note that it is usual to record the 'actual' amounts, once they are known, in a column next to the budgeted. Obviously, subsequent months' budget figures must be adjusted for any differences between the estimated and the actual.

An accurate cash budget is essential to good management, and is one of the documents which *must* be attached to any business plan. It is usually prepared on a 'rolling plan' basis – that is, an extra month is added as each month is completed, so that one is always looking (say) six months ahead. It has three main objectives:

(a) it provides objectives to work to (for example, estimating the income implies setting targets for sales);

(b) it monitors actual performance (for example, it can alert a manager to the fact that debtors are not paying their debts as quickly as had been expected);

(c) it focuses attention on likely problems or situations calling for action (for example, if the budget throws up the possibility of a cash deficit in three months' time, then action can be taken in good time to avert the problem, such as obtaining bank overdraft facilities. Just as important will be the best utilisation of anticipated surpluses.

SOME PARTICULAR ACCOUNTING PROBLEMS 113

The difficulty of any estimate is that of coming up with figures which are reasonably reliable. There is no easy answer to this one, except very careful enquiry and planning.

TOWARDS YOUR BUSINESS PLAN

1 Identify the types of insurance which you think your firm should have.

Obtain and file as much information about the different policies as possible.

What will be the probable annual cost?

2 Do you anticipate employing a number of staff? What are your plans for handling the pay roll and the wage payment procedures?

3 Do you anticipate that your firm will be subject to VAT? If so, what arrangements do you intend to make?

4 Prepare a cash budget showing the anticipated cash receipts and payments of your firm, in as much detail as possible, over the next (or over its first) six months. What problems does it show up? Note down the actions which will be necessary in respect of these.

The Business Plan

If you have followed through the ten big questions, and built up your file with the information suggested at the end of each section, you should now be in an excellent position to prepare a formal business plan.

The business plan is where we get down to specifics in relation to a proposed business or a new project. And it must be *specific* – no room here for the 'probably', and the 'round about', and the 'I think so' type of reply. If you have not refined the information required down to the definite, to the sort of statement you can justify objectively, then you had better start working on it. Because nothing less is good enough for a business plan.

A business plan is a formal document which sets out *in detail* the relevant information for a business proposal. The more important objectives of a business plan include:

(a) clarifying your own ideas about what you want to do, and the feasibility of doing it;

(b) identifying likely problem areas where you will need to undertake further investigation, or will have to seek professional support and help;

(c) setting objectives;

(d) acting as a monitor of progress towards reaching those objectives;

(e) establishing an action plan;

(f) supporting applications for financial and other help.

BLUEPRINT OF A BUSINESS PLAN

The need for specific, objective statements has already been emphasised. In addition, the plan must be set out coherently and logically under clear heads and subheads. Supporting detail can be attached to the main plan in the form of clearly numbered and labelled appendices. Several copies should be prepared and advantage should be taken of the wide range of files and wallets now on the market in order to bind the pages together. Indeed, the whole plan must have the professional touch about its presentation and format – it may well be worthwhile seeking the services of a secretarial agency in this connection.

There is no set form or pattern for a business plan, though some items should clearly precede others. The following blueprint is suggested as a guide – it should be modified in whatever way necessary to suit the specific needs and demands of a particular business.

1 Header

e.g. *Business Plan for Sunshades Ltd*
October 1988.

Remember that your business plan may be filed with others – maybe it will be left lying around with other documents of a quite different nature – and anyone picking it up is going to want to see at a glance what the document is all about and to whom it refers.

2 Background

- The proposed name of the firm
- Contact address and telephone number (if any)
- Brief description of the type of product or service to be offered
- Actual or intended date of commencement of business
- Name and address of each promoter, together with brief mention of qualifications and experience – both general and that relevant to the product to be offered

3 The proposed firm

- The legal format proposed for the firm (sole

proprietorship, partnership, company) together with steps taken or enquiries made to date
- The official address of the firm (if decided)

4 The Product

- Precise nature of the product(s) or service(s) to be offered
- Evidence of the demand for the product in the area concerned
- Analysis of raw materials, components, other stocks likely to be needed
- List of potential suppliers with details of any approach or arrangement already made with them

5 Premises and equipment

- Nature and location of premises acquired/likely to be needed. Proposed method of acquisition – freehold, leasehold, etc., including notes on security of tenure
- Equipment likely to be needed, plus plans for its acquisition
  - factory/workshop equipment
  - office equipment
  - other (e.g. motor vehicles)
- Analysis of special operating skills will be needed
- Note on maintenance proposals
- Note on depreciation and replacement problems

5 Marketing plans

- Detailed statement of likely sales levels by week/month or other appropriate period
- Stock
  - levels to be held
  - storage problems

- Estimated revenue from sales
- Estimated costs and break-even points
- Statement regarding present/likely competition
- Description of credit
  - likely to be obtained from suppliers
  - likely to be taken by debtors
- Proposed channels of distribution of product (where applicable)
- Proposed advertising plans

6 Trading and other stocks

- Analysis of requirements by item, quantity and cost of raw materials; trading goods; spare parts and maintenance supplies; stationery supplies.
- Proposals for storage and stock control

7 Staffing

- Analysis of staff requirements (i) short-term (ii) long-term
- Training needs and proposals
- Anticipated costs

8 Finance

- Calculation of capital needed for
  - start-up
  - survival period
  - normal operational requirements
- Proposed sources
- Repayment proposals in respect of borrowed finance

9 Accounting

- Summary of accounting system proposed
- Note on position regarding VAT, tax and social insurance

- Note on credit terms and control; bad debts procedures
- Estimated profit and loss forecasts for the foreseeable future
- Estimated cash budget for foreseeable future

10 Specialised services
- Discussions with specialised agencies
  - summary of discussions already taken place
  - note of proposed consultations

11 The immediate future
- Outline of anticipated but currently unresolved problems
- Outline of action plan for getting the firm off the ground

HELPLINE 6

Once you have established your business...

Once your have prepared your Business Plan, the real hard work – that of actually establishing your business – will begin. Once you are 'in the fray', you may find the services of the following organisations which specialise in meeting the needs of existing small businesses helpful:

Association of Independent Businesses
Trowbay House, 108 Weston Street, London SE1 3QB
(01 403 4066)
Run by practising business men. Seeks through direct links with government to improve the political and economic climate for independent businesses. Offers advice, discounts and other services.

National Federation of Self-employed and Small Businesses
32 St Anne's Road West, Lytham St Annes, Lancs FY8 1NY (0253 720911)

A strong pressure group representing the interests of self-employed persons and owners of small businesses. Offers a range of services; membership privileges include legal insurance covering representation at VAT tribunals, Health and Safety prosecutions, and motoring prosecutions.

The Small Business Bureau
32 Smith Square, London SW1P 3HH (01 222 0330)
Primarily a lobby group seeking legislation to make for a better climate for small businesses. Produces the Small Business *monthly newspaper which incorporates tax news. Has a special* Women into Business *section running seminars and producing bi-monthly newspaper by women for women.*

INDEX

Accounting
  cash 90–101
  and computers 49–51, 91
  systems 90–93
Acts of Parliament
  Companies 69, 74, 76
  Consumer Credit 87–88
  Data Protection 62
  Finance (1986) 71
  Financial Services 105
  Health and Safety at Work 11, 47–48
  Industrial and Provident Societies 71
  Landlord and Tenant 30
  Limited Partnership 68
  Partnership 67
Advertising 19–20
  for staff 57–58
Annual Percentage Rate of Return (APR) 88
Articles of association 77
Association of Independent Businesses 118
Audit 110

Bank(s)
  loans 83
  statements and reconciliations 102–103
British Insurance and Investment Brokers Association (BIIBA) 66, 105, 109
Budgets 110–113
Business(es)
  directories 12, 15
  home-based 24–25
  plans 114–119
  purchase of existing 11, 23, 35

Capital
  loan 78
  needs 10, 81
  repayment holiday 84
  share 77–78
  sources 81–87
  venture 83
Car parking 27–28
Cash budgeting 110–113
Chambers of Trade and Commerce 15
Company(ies) 69, 74–79
  audit of 110
  close 76
  Registrar 76
  Registration Office 79
Computer(isation) 37–38, 49–51, 91
Co-operative(s) 69–72
  Advisory Group 70
  Bank 70
  College 70
  Development Agency 71, 72
  Union 72
CoSIRA – *see* Rural Development Commission Business Service
Credit 8
Crime prevention 36–37
Customs and Excise 107

Dalton's Weekly 31
Data Protection Office 62
Delivery notes 38
Demand levels 16–17
Department of Employment 86–87
Distribution channels 18–19

Engineering 11
Enterprise
  allowance schemes 85
  zones 85–86
Environmental health 48

Fire prevention 36–37
Franchise(ing) 12, 35

Health and Safety
  Commission/Executive 48–49, 60, 61
Hire purchase 53
Home – working from 24–25
Hotel and catering 10

Image of firm 17–18
Import/export businesses 10

Industrial Common Owner Finance Ltd (ICOF) 70, 85
Industrial Common Ownership Movement (ICOM) 70
Industrial Training Boards (ITB) 56
Information Technology Centres (ITEC) 50
Insurance 109–110
  national 59, 76, 105
  of premises 24
Interviewing 58–59

Kalamazoo 93

Labour availability 27
Leasing 52–53
Legal forms of business 64–72
Lighting, heating 25
Limited liability 74–75
Loans Guarantee Unit 87
Local authority services 84
Location 27
Logos 18
Maintenance (equipment) 45–46
Manpower Services Commission (MSC) 56, 87
Manufacturing 11
Market research 14, 15
Marketing 14–20
Memorandum of association 77

Name – of product/firm 17–18
National Federation of Self Employed 118
National insurance 59, 76, 105
  and DHSS 65

Order form 38

Partner(ships) 66–69, 83
Pension 66
Police and security 36–37
Premises
  purchase of 29–30
  requirements of 25–29
Product
  which to offer 9–11
  marketability 7–13
Production, volume of 20
Purchase
  of assets 52
  of premises 29–30

Qualifications 9
Questions, the preliminary 2–6

References and testimonials 61–62
Rental of premises 30
Restrictive covenants 24
Retailing 10
Rural Development Commission Business Service (RDCBS) 15–16, 31, 35, 44, 84, 87

Safety 11, 47–49
Share capital 77–78
Skills 9–10
Small Business Bureau 119
Small Business Service 15, 31, 35, 44, 84–85
Sole proprietorships 64–66
Staffing
  conditions of employment 59–62
  needs 55–56
  recruitment 57–59
Stock
  and computers 49–51
  control 33–42
  control budget 40–41
  re-order levels 40–42
Stores register 38–40
Stress 4

Tax
  advance corporation 75
  capital gains 24
  and companies 75–76
  deductions 60, 75, 105
  and partnerships 68–69
  publications 65, 108
  value added 35, 106–108
Telephone 25–6
Temperature
  of premises 25
Trade associations 15

Value added tax (VAT) 35, 106–108

Wage procedures 103–106
Waste disposal 26–27
Wordprocessing 49, 51

Yellow Pages 12, 15, 31, 35